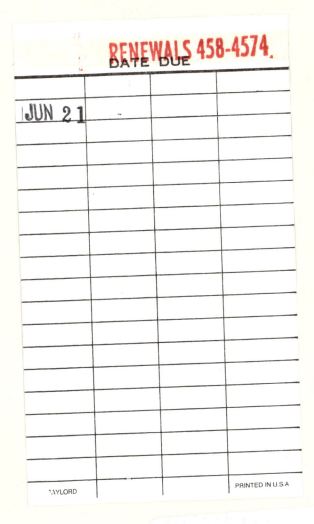

GAYLORD

PRINTED IN U.S.A

D0222379

Series/Number 07-76

LONGITUDINAL RESEARCH
Second Edition

SCOTT MENARD
Institute of Behavioral Science
University of Colorado, Boulder

 SAGE PUBLICATIONS
International Educational and Professional Publisher
Thousand Oaks   London   New Delhi

For information:

 Sage Publications, Inc.
2455 Teller Road
Thousand Oaks, California 91320
E-mail: order@sagepub.com

Sage Publications Ltd.
6 Bonhill Street
London EC2A 4PU
United Kingdom

Sage Publications India Pvt. Ltd.
M-32 Market
Greater Kailash I
New Delhi 110 048 India

Printed in the United States of America

Library of Congress Cataloging-in-Publication Data

Menard, Scott W.
  Longitudinal research / by Scott Menard.—2nd ed.
     p. cm.—(Sage university papers series. Quantitative
applications in the social sciences; no. 07-76)
Includes bibliographical references.
  ISBN 0-7619-2209-1 (pbk.)
  1. Social sciences—Longitudinal studies. I. Title. II. Series.
  H62 .M39 2002
  300´.7´2—dc211

                                                    2002005572

02   03   10   9   8   7   6   5   4   3   2   1

Acquiring Editor:	C. Deborah Laughton
Editorial Assistant:	Veronica Novak
Production Editor:	Diana E. Axelsen
Copy Editor:	Linda Gray
Typesetter:	C&M Digitals (P) Ltd., Chennai, India

CONTENTS

SERIES EDITOR'S INTRODUCTION

Cross-sectional research examines data from a point in time, whereas longitudinal research examines data from across time. In a typical cross-sectional study, the variables are measured once on each case, during the same period. An example would be a public opinion survey of eligible voters, held just before the 2000 presidential election. In a typical longitudinal study, the variables are measured repeatedly over different periods. An example would be a public opinion survey of the same eligible voters, asked the same questions twice, before the 1996 and 2000 presidential elections. The second design, called a "panel," would be much more costly than the ordinary cross-sectional survey. Is the extra cost worth it? Yes, if the goal is to measure change and, more broadly, more firmly forge the chain of causality.

Suppose Professor Mary Brown, a political scientist, was interested in economic voting theory, namely, how change in a voter's personal economic circumstance influences changing support for the president's party. In our hypothetical panel study, say that respondents were asked to report their finances and their vote, in time 1 (1996) and time 2 (2000). These change scores (time 1 score – time 2 score) represent real change in attitudes and behavior. Furthermore, because of the temporal sequencing, they make possible stronger inferences about how changes in economic circumstances can lead to vote change. With respect to making a causal argument, such panel evidence would be much stronger than cross-sectional evidence, which records no real change at all.

The panel is just one type of longitudinal design and in fact can be divided into prospective and retrospective. Various design types are nicely described in the second edition of Professor Menard's useful monograph. Besides the panel, there are the total population, the repeated cross-sectional, and the revolving panel designs. With a total population design the population is repeatedly measured, for example, the U.S. Census. In a repeated cross-sectional design, the population is sampled independently and repeatedly, for example, the American National Election Studies. In a revolving panel design, the population is repeatedly sampled, with subsamples added or dropped after several periods, for example, the National Crime Survey. Depending on the design, longitudinal data gathering poses vi

special problems. For instance, with a panel, attrition of cases can be serious. When the measures of the variables change from one period to the next, inference can become difficult. Missing data treatment appears especially complex in overtime studies. These issues, as well as others, are carefully discussed in this monograph.

Analysis of longitudinal data can be complicated, but Professor Menard's explication makes the going much easier. The preferred analysis strategy is partly determined by the shape of the data set, in terms of number of cases and periods. Few cases and many periods characterize most time series, which generally require some version of an autoregression adjustment procedure. By way of contrast, many cases and few periods characterize most panels, which may be analyzed with change scores or a lagged endogenous variable. The creation of new longitudinal analysis procedures is a growth area in social science methods, as more and more overtime data become available. The Menard monograph provides a readable introduction to this investigative style, which seems preferred whenever the scholar has a question about developmental trends, historical change, attitude evolution, or dynamic processes.

—*Michael S. Lewis-Beck*

PREFACE TO THE SECOND EDITION

Since I finished writing the first edition of this monograph in 1990, a great deal has changed in the field of longitudinal research, especially in longitudinal data analysis. As McArdle and Bell (2000: 69-70) put it, "During the 1990s, many methodologists have added to the knowledge base, and longitudinal methods have enjoyed a remarkable period of growth–hardly a day goes by without 'new' and 'improved' methods sprouting up." Well, maybe the progress hasn't been quite that rapid, but it has been substantial. The decade of the 1990s saw the publication of Bryk and Raudenbush (1992), whose book along with their HLM program revolutionized our approach to analyzing multilevel and longitudinal data. There are references to latent growth curve modeling using structural equation modeling (SEM) programs prior to 1990 (e.g., Jöreskog & Sörbom, 1989:261-266), but in the 1990s, latent growth curve models were widely adopted for modeling intraindividual change using SEM. Discussions of alternative ways of dealing with missing data also precede the past decade, but the 1990s have seen an increasing focus on more sophisticated approaches to dealing with missing data in both cross-sectional and longitudinal research. Software applicable to longitudinal research has also improved, and more evidence for the rapid pace of change in longitudinal analysis can be found in the dozen or so books written and edited about longitudinal research design and data analysis published in the 1990s and early in the present millennium.

The organization of this monograph remains the same as in the first edition. The material in the first four chapters has been updated to include more recent research in these areas, but it should seem familiar to readers of the first edition. Material on temporal and causal order has been consolidated at the end of Chapter 2. Chapter 5, on longitudinal analysis, has been almost completely rewritten, reflecting the progress that has been made in longitudinal data analysis over the past decade or so. There is much less said about the application of traditional methods of analysis to longitudinal data, and more focus on analytical methods specifically designed for longitudinal data, including time series analysis, linear panel analysis, multilevel and latent growth curve modeling, and event history analysis. The description of these methods remains brief, as in the first edition, but includes citations to sources with more detailed coverage of these topics.

ACKNOWLEDGMENTS

I am grateful once again to Delbert S. Elliott, Frank M. Andrews, and an anonymous reviewer for their helpful comments and suggestions on the first edition; also to Steven Finkel and Peter V. Marsden for their thoughtful and constructive reviews of this second edition; to Zeke Little for some of the original graphics; and to Michael Lewis-Beck, the series editor, and C. Deborah Laughton, editor at Sage Publications, for their continued encouragement and support.

LONGITUDINAL RESEARCH

Scott Menard
Institute of Behavioral Science
University of Colorado, Boulder

1. INTRODUCTION

Longitudinal data have been collected at the national level for more than 300 years, beginning with the periodic censuses taken by New France (Canada) and continued in Quebec from 1665 until 1754. These were not the first censuses, but they did represent the first periodic collection of census data, as opposed to single, isolated censuses taken at irregular intervals, the latter beginning as early as the Israelite census of 1491 B.C. (Thomlinson, 1976). Other periodic censuses that have continued to the present include those of Sweden since 1749, Norway and Denmark since 1769, and the United States since 1790. The United States is exceptional among nations because it has longitudinal census data from the first decade of its existence as a nation up to the present. At the individual level, Baltes and Nesselroade (1979) and Wall and Williams (1970) cite collection of longitudinal data (primarily case study and biographical data) as early as 1759. Long-term studies of childhood development involving multiple subjects flourished in the United States after World War I, and a broad array of longitudinal studies in the social and behavioral sciences has been undertaken since the 1970s. The proliferation of longitudinal research attests to its perceived importance by both researchers and major funding agencies. When questions have been raised about the value of longitudinal research, those questions have more often addressed the quality of the research in terms of design and analysis than the value of longitudinal research in principle for answering questions that cannot adequately be addressed by other types of data collection designs and analyses.

For many, longitudinal research is touted as a panacea for establishing temporal order, measuring change, and making stronger causal interpretations. Although there are indeed certain advantages associated with these methods, there are offsetting costs and difficulties. Longitudinal research may not always be necessary even for establishing causal order (Blalock, 1962; Davis, 1985), particularly when the temporal order of variables is known in advance (e.g., biological or genetic characteristics such as sex,

1

race, and age), and longitudinal data are certainly not a cure for weak research design and data analysis.

Definition

In the present discussion of longitudinal research, I use the term *longitudinal* to describe not a single method, but a family of methods (Zazzo, 1967, cited in Wall & Williams, 1970). This family of methods is best understood by contrasting longitudinal research with cross-sectional research. In *pure cross-sectional research* measurement occurs once for each individual, subject, country, or *case* in the study; the measurement of each item, concept, or *variable* applies to a single time interval or *period*; and the measurement of each variable for each case occurs within a sufficiently narrow span of time (ideally it would occur simultaneously for each variable for each case) that the measurements may be regarded as *contemporaneous*, that is, occurring within the same period for all variables and for all cases. Depending on the particular study, a period may be defined in terms of seconds, days, months, years, or (in principle) geological epochs. In the social and behavioral sciences, periods typically vary from minutes in some laboratory experiments to decades in some cross-national research.

Longitudinal research must be defined in terms of both the data and the methods of analysis used in the research. Longitudinal research is research in which (a) data are collected for each item or variable for two or more distinct time periods; (b) the subjects or cases analyzed are the same or at least comparable from one period to the next; and (c) the analysis involves some comparison of data between or among periods. At a bare minimum, any truly longitudinal design would permit the measurement of differences or change in a variable from one period to another. According to this definition, several types of research may be regarded as longitudinal. In one, data may be collected *at* two or more distinct periods, *for* those distinct periods, on the same set of cases and variables in each period. This is a *prospective panel design*. Alternatively, data may be collected *at* a single period *for* several periods, usually including the period that ends with the time at which the data are collected. This *retrospective panel design* may be identical to a prospective panel design in every respect except the number of times data collection actually takes place and the length of the recall period required of respondents. In both panel designs the cases and variables remain the same from one period to the next. A third possibility is to collect data on the same set of variables for (and perhaps *at*) two or more periods but to include nonidentical (but comparable) cases in each period. In this *repeated cross-sectional design*, the data for each period may be regarded as a separate cross-section, but because the cases are comparable from one period to another (e.g., by using probability samples drawn from the same population), we may make comparisons between or among periods. These different types of longitudinal designs are presented in greater detail in Chapter 3.

Baltes and Nesselroade (1979) and Wall and Williams (1970) have suggested narrower definitions of longitudinal research that would exclude all except prospective panel designs, but they acknowledge (Baltes & Nesselroade, 1979, p. 4; Wall & Williams, 1970, p. 14) that there is no consensus on this point. Baltes and Nesselroade suggest that longitudinal research may need to be defined within the context of a specific discipline. For developmental studies in psychology, it may be appropriate to consider only longitudinal panel designs, but in other disciplines this seems too restrictive. Reasons for using a broader definition of longitudinal research are, first, the lack of consensus regarding what constitutes longitudinal research, and second, the usefulness of considering the different features of the full range of methods used in collecting data for different time periods.

The remainder of this monograph is organized as follows. In Chapter 2, the purposes of longitudinal research and the difficulties involved in separating historical and developmental changes are discussed. Chapter 3 presents and discusses basic designs for the collection of longitudinal data. In Chapter 4, issues that may affect the quality of longitudinal data are discussed. Finally, a brief introduction to and overview of methods of longitudinal analysis are presented in Chapter 5.

2. THE PURPOSES OF LONGITUDINAL RESEARCH

Longitudinal research serves two primary purposes: to describe patterns of change and to establish the direction (positive or negative and from Y to X or from X to Y) and magnitude (a relationship of magnitude zero indicating the absence of a causal relationship) of causal relationships. Change is typically measured with reference to one of two continua: chronological time (hereafter simply *time*) or *age*. Time is measured externally to the cases or subjects being studied (e.g., 2:22 P.M., August 28, 2000). Age is measured internally, relative to the subject or case under study (e.g., 38 years, 7 months, 26 days, 8 hours, and 27 minutes since birth). In one sense, age represents biological time for human subjects. The choice of time or age as the underlying continuum may be important, and for some purposes it may be useful to consider both in the same analysis. Also important is the distinction between age-related differences when age is measured cross-sectionally (differences between subjects who are 40 years old and subjects who are 50 years old in 1990) and age measured longitudinally (differences between subjects who are 40 years old in 1990 and those same subjects when they are 50 years old in 2000). When age is measured cross-sectionally, the differences between variables for 40-year-olds and 50-year-olds may be interpreted as differences *between* birth cohorts or age groups at a particular time. When age is measured longitudinally, the differences may be interpreted as *developmental* differences *within* a cohort or age group over time.

Age, Period, and Cohort Effects

The distinction between time and age as conceptually distinct continua along which change may be measured can pose serious problems of interpretation in the study of change. To understand these problems, and to lay a firm foundation for discussing the measurement of historical and developmental change, it is necessary to discuss the distinctions among age, period, and cohort effects, and the different conceptual statuses of age, period, and cohort as variables and as units of analysis.

The demographic definition of a cohort is provided by Glenn (1977:8): "A cohort is defined as those people within a geographically or otherwise delineated population who experienced the same significant life event within a given period of time." A similar definition is offered by Ryder (1965). Both Glenn and Ryder note that although the term *cohort* is almost always used to refer to *birth* cohorts (those born in a particular year or period), one may also define cohorts in terms of year of marriage or divorce, year of retirement or first employment, year of entry into or graduation from college or graduate school, or year of occurrence of any number of events other than birth. Graetz (1987) uses the term *event cohort* to describe cohorts other than birth cohorts.

Suppose that we want to test the hypothesis that people become politically more conservative as they grow older. One approach would be to do a survey of individuals of different ages in a given year, ask questions about their political attitudes, and compare younger respondents with older respondents. If the older respondents reported being more politically conservative than the younger respondents, we might conclude that people do become more conservative as they get older, but there is a plausible alternative hypothesis. Perhaps those in our sample who are older and more conservative were just as conservative when they were younger, and perhaps our younger, less conservative respondents will remain less conservative as they grow older. In other words, cross-sectional differences by age may be confused with differences that result not from age but from the effects of membership in different birth cohorts. Put another way, different life experiences at certain, perhaps relatively young, ages may have long-lasting effects on the attitudes of different individuals.

Suppose now that instead of doing a cross-sectional study, we select a single birth cohort and interview a sample of respondents from this cohort every 5 or 10 years until they die. At the end of our study, if we found that respondents were more conservative when they were older, we might conclude that political conservatism increases with age. Again, however, there is a plausible alternative hypothesis. It is possible that there is no real difference among age groups in any one year but that everyone, young and old, is becoming more conservative over time, for reasons that have nothing to do with age. This would suggest an effect of history, specific to years or periods rather than to ages. Put another way, contemporary events may have an immediate effect on political conservatism, regardless of age. The problem of a period difference does not arise in the cross-sectional study because there is only one period. The problem of a cohort difference does not arise in the single-cohort longitudinal study because there is only one cohort.

Since neither a cross-sectional study nor a single-cohort longitudinal study can eliminate both cohort membership and period effects as rival hypotheses, it would seem logical to combine the two approaches and use a multiple-year, multiple-cohort design. Then we could control for both cohort membership and period in examining the effect of age on political conservatism. The problem with this is that if we assume that the effects of age, period, and cohort membership are all linear, controlling for any two variables controls for the third as well. This is because age, period, and cohort membership, as measured here, are linearly dependent; each is a linear function of the other two. Mathematically,

cohort (year of birth) = period (calendar year) – age (years since birth).

Again we are stymied in our attempt to test the hypothesis that political conservatism increases as a result of age. Including all three (age, period, and cohort) in a regression equation, for example, would result in perfect collinearity. Any age effect we find without controlling for both period and cohort may, with equal plausibility, be attributable to the combined or separate effects of cohort membership and trends over time. This problem, along with other problems in cohort analysis (sampling, sample mortality, etc.) is discussed in some detail in Glenn (1977).

Linear Dependence and the Conceptual Status of Cohorts. Attempts have been made to overcome the problem of linear dependence among age, period, and birth cohort. These include the use of dummy-variable regression analysis with certain restrictive assumptions about the parameters in the model (Mason et al., 1973) and the recombination and a priori elimination of one or more of the three types of effects (Palmore, 1978). These attempts, particularly the dummy-variable regression model, have generated considerable methodological controversy (Baltes et al., 1979; Glenn, 1976, 1977; Knoke & Hout, 1976; Mason et al., 1976; Rodgers 1982a, 1982b; Smith et al., 1982) regarding the plausibility of the assumptions and the consequences of violating the assumptions needed to deal with the problem of linear dependence among age, period, and birth cohort. Although constraints in the dummy-variable regression models can eliminate the problem of perfect collinearity, the dummy variables used in the model typically remain highly collinear, and slightly different constraints can produce very different substantive conclusions. In addition, these methods do not solve the problem of linear dependence, because the Mason et al. (1973) model assumes that not all the effects are linear, and in Palmore's method, one effect must be eliminated a priori.

Note that the problem of linear dependence applies to birth cohorts, but not necessarily to other types of cohorts. To the extent that an event is not dependent on age or period, an event cohort based on that event is not linearly dependent on age or period. In some cases, then, linear dependence may be eliminated a priori. A second and more fundamental point regarding age, period, and cohort effects is that *cohorts, as aggregates of individuals, are units of analysis*, cases for study. It is in this sense that the term cohort is used by Ryder (1965) and implemented in some studies of cohort effects (e.g., Carlson, 1979; Lloyd et al., 1987; Wetzel et al., 1987). Baltes et al. (1979) discuss three possible conceptualizations of cohort (error or disturbance; dimension of generalization; theoretical and process variable), one of which (dimension of generalization) corresponds to the use of cohorts as units of analysis rather than as theoretical variables. Even some studies that use cohort as an explanatory variable also recognize cohort as a unit of analysis (e.g., Wright & Maxim, 1987).

Cohorts are aggregates of individuals (cases). As cases, they may be analyzed in the same way as other cases (individuals, cities, nations). In social science research, cohorts, like other aggregate cases, have measurable characteristics, some of which are inherently aggregate in nature (size, sex ratio, ethnic composition) and others of which are summations (total number of arrests) or averages (median lifetime income) of the individuals who are included in the cohort. By contrast, we do not measure aggregate characteristics of ages or periods as such, but we may measure aggregate characteristics of cases *during* a particular age or period. Ages and periods are aggregates of time, variables rather than units of analysis. They may be used to delimit the cases for analysis in a particular study, but they are not themselves typically employed as units of analysis in social research.

Age, period, and birth cohort, respectively, answer the questions, "How old are you?" "What year is it?" and "In what year were you born?" The answer to the question, "How old are you?" may explain some forms of behavior: wetting one's pants is most common in infancy, illegal behavior tends to be highest in adolescence, and retirement is most common after age 65. Age provides a *developmental* explanation for behavior. The answer to the question. "What year is it?" may also help explain some forms of behavior: In the United States, use of illicit drugs was more common after 1960 than before, and overt racial discrimination was more common before 1960 than after. Period provides an explanation, or at least a weak proxy for an explanation (Hobcraft et al., 1982), that is *historical* in nature and that may help identify those historical events that are most plausible as explanations for a given behavior.

There are two ways in which the answer to the question, "In what year were you born?" may be used to explain behavior. The first is what we may call Oriental Astrological Theory: individuals born in certain years have certain characteristics by virtue of having been born in that year. For example, according to Oriental astrology, women born in the year of the fiery horse (which recurs every 60 years) have a propensity to murder their husbands. For most social scientists, this is a rather unsatisfactory approach to explaining homicide; it does, however, have an impact either on actual fertility or on the reported (but not necessarily true) birth date of women in Japan, as documented by the Population Reference Bureau (1989). Alternatively, the year in which one is born explains one's behavior in terms of how old one was (development) in a particular year or during particular events (history). In other words, the effect of birth cohort, measured as year of birth, may serve as a proxy for the interaction of the effects of age and period.

Cohort Effects: Reconceptualization and Replacement. One approach to cohort effects, then, is to regard them as the interaction of age and period effects. An alternative would be to assume that it is not cohort membership itself but, rather, some characteristic or set of characteristics associated with the birth cohort that produced the apparent cohort effect. The problem then becomes one of identifying the appropriate characteristic or set of characteristics of the cohort, a theoretical rather than a methodological problem.

One solution to this problem has potentially broad applicability: For cohort, measured as year of birth, substitute the number of individuals born in a birth cohort, or cohort size. According to Ryder (1965:845), "A cohort's size relative to its neighbors is a persistent and compelling feature of its lifetime environment." Mason et al. (1976:905) note that all three variables—age, period, and cohort—are proxies for unmeasured variables, and they indicate that "if cohort size is the variable which causes differentiation in the context of a specific substantive problem, then, if size measurements can be constructed, it is unnecessary to include cohorts as such in the specification because the preferred variable is available." They also note that use of cohort size eliminates the estimability problem for which their dummy variable regression model was constructed and makes the results of the analysis less tentative. Hobcraft et al. (1982) and Rodgers (1982a) raise similar points. Ryder (1965) notes that size is only one of several characteristics that may be used to differentiate cohorts from one another; however, cohort size is the characteristic that has played the most important role in research since the publication in 1968 of Easterlin's work regarding the impact of cohort size on the labor force, and his subsequent work, published in 1980, regarding the impact of cohort size on a variety of social problems, including unemployment, divorce, and crime (Easterlin, 1987).

The point of all this is that cohort, measured as year of birth, has sometimes been used when cohort size or some other cohort characteristic (or a nonlinear interaction term involving age and period) would have been more conceptually or theoretically appropriate for studying age, period, and cohort effects. This may stem at least in part from a failure to recognize that age, period, and cohort have qualitatively different conceptual statuses. Although, as noted above, cohort membership may be treated as an explanatory variable from a purely methodological viewpoint, theoretically and substantively it is not generally appropriate to do so. Age and period are more appropriate as explanatory variables, age more so than period (Hobcraft et al., 1982). Ideally, one would eliminate period and cohort and replace them with the variables for which they act as proxies in any causal analysis.

In the analysis of developmental or historical change, the use of multiple-year, multiple-cohort designs, coupled with appropriate operationalization of age, period, and cohort effects (i.e., the use of cohort characteristics or of a nonlinear age-period interaction) would allow us to test whether age had an effect on political attitudes, net of period effects and cohort membership. Some solution of the problem of confounding among age, period, and cohort effects, whether theoretical (e.g., use of cohort size based on the work of Easterlin and others, or a priori elimination of the possibility of a cohort effect) or methodological (e.g., use of the Mason et al. dummy variable regression technique), needs to be found before age effects can be inferred in any study. In the example of political conservatism, it may be theoretically reasonable to eliminate cohort membership as an influence on political attitudes or to assume (on theoretical grounds) that any effect of cohort membership operates through cohort size (or some other cohort characteristic). Once this is done, it becomes possible to estimate separate age (developmental) and period (historical) effects on political attitudes. Note that developmental, historical, and cohort membership effects cannot be clearly separated without longitudinal data.

Period Effects: Changes Over Time. Once one has dealt with the issue of separating age, period, and cohort effects, it becomes possible to examine changes as they occur over time. Typically, this will mean either ignoring cohort effects or representing them in terms of cohort characteristics such as cohort size. In addition, if we are concerned only with changes over chronological time (historical changes) and not with changes over age (developmental changes), we must either be certain that age is entirely irrelevant or include age as an explanatory variable or control for age by making age-specific comparisons.

One concern of longitudinal research is the simple description of changes in values of variables over time. At the individual level of analysis, this may include changes in religious beliefs, political conservatism, or use of alcohol. Most often, it is necessary to consider the possibility that change at the individual level may represent a developmental rather than a historical trend. At an aggregate level, we may use changes in rates of crime or victimization, in worker productivity or in per capita gross national product, in Scholastic Aptitude Test (SAT) scores or in infant mortality rates, as *social indicators*[1] of progress or decline in meeting basic social needs or achieving desirable social goals. At this level, it may be possible to control for the effects of age. Infant mortality is already age specific (although the age of the mother may affect the likelihood of the infant's death before age 1), and the SAT is taken primarily by individuals aged 16 to 18. Age is thus controlled completely or to a large extent for these measures. Rates of crime and victimization are sensitive to the age distribution of the population (e.g., Chilton & Spielberger, 1971; Skogan, 1976), and it would be appropriate to control for age composition in evaluating the evidence for historical trends in these variables. Per capita gross national product may be sensitive to the age-dependency ratio (the ratio of those under age 15 plus those over age 65 to those aged 16-64), and it is also possible that worker productivity is sensitive to the age distribution of workers, but if these change slowly or remain fairly constant over the periods for which the data are collected, it may be possible to ignore changes in age or age distribution as sources of variation in period trends.

One of the safest ways to approach the study of trends over time is to use age-specific comparisons. In an age-specific comparison, only those cases of a certain age in one year are compared with cases of the same age in some subsequent year. The age may represent a single year (e.g., age 15) or a range of years (e.g., over age 65), and separate comparisons may be made for all possible ages or age groups. For example, Gold and his associates (Gold & Reimer, 1975; Williams & Gold, 1972) examined rates of self-reported delinquency among national probability samples of 13- to 16-year-olds in a repeated cross-sectional design and found little evidence of change from 1967 to 1972. Menard (1987b) obtained similar results for national probability samples of 15- to 17-year-olds from 1976 to 1980. Covey and Menard (1987, 1988) examined trends in victimization and trends in arrests for those over age 65 and found that rates of arrests were generally increasing and rates of victimization were generally decreasing among this older age group. In each of the above-cited studies, controlling for age produced relatively unambiguous evidence for the existence or absence of trends over time. Without such controls for age, it may be difficult to ascertain whether changes are historical or developmental in nature, even if the entire population is used instead of a sample. Chilton and Spielberger (1971) examined changes in official crime rates and found that much of the apparent change over time (what appeared on the surface to be a change in behavior) was attributable to changes in the age structure, or more specifically, to changes in the percentage of the population in the adolescent ages. Individual studies will vary, but in general, it is appropriate to consider the possibility that apparent period trends may actually be attributable to changes in age (at the individual level) or age composition (at the aggregate level).

Historical Trends in Relationships Between Variables. Another concern of longitudinal research is the examination of changes, not in values or levels of variables over time, but in relationships between or among variables over time. It is one thing, for example, to say that mortality has been declining for over two centuries. It is another to indicate that in the early stages of mortality decline, reductions in mortality were achieved primarily by public health measures (sanitation, access to safe drinking water, pasteurization, etc.) and that medicine played little if any role, but in the later stages of the decline, advances in medicine (inoculation, antibiotics) rather than public health measures were responsible for mortality declines (McKeown, 1976; McKeown & Record, 1962; McNeill, 1976). Hout et al. (1999) examined the relationship between social class (six categories, from professional to less skilled blue collar) and voting behavior in American presidential elections from 1944 to 1992 and found different patterns for different classes. The tendency of the highest (professional) class to support Republican candidates increased over time, while the tendency of the three lower socioeconomic classes to vote Democratic declined over time, particularly for the nonprofessional self-employed and the skilled manual classes.

In the context of examining changes in the strength or patterns of relationships over time, one important concern is the replication of previous results with new data. Elliott et al. (1989) used data from successive years to test a theoretical model of delinquent behavior on a set of dependent variables that included delinquency, drug use, and mental health problems. In the initial test, the results indicated that the model did a good job of explaining delinquency and drug use but a poorer job of explaining mental health problems. Using data from the same subjects, measured 1 year later, Elliott et al. successfully replicated the results of the first test. The ability to replicate results from one period to the next (in effect, an indicator of reliability of results) provides more support for the model than would a single test, without replication.

Replication is not always successful, and evidence of changes in strength or patterns of relationships over time may alert the researcher to real changes in relationships or to methodological problems such as instability or unreliability of measurement, or misspecification of a causal model. Menard (1987a) tested a model of fertility on 85 less developed countries for the periods 1970 and 1980. The overall patterns for the two periods were very similar, but relationships involving family planning program effort changed from 1970 to 1980, usually in the direction of weaker relationships. Other than this change, the models for the two periods produced almost identical results. As indicated by Menard, these changes may have reflected changes in the measurement of family planning program effort, but the strong relationship (Pearson's $r = .83$) between family planning program effort as measured in the two periods seemed more suggestive of a real change in the strength of the relationship than of unreliability in measurement. Neither the possibility of instability or unreliability of measurement nor the overall consistency of the model from one period to another could have been documented without replication.

Age Effects: Life Cycle and Developmental Changes. Baltes and Nesselroade (1979) listed five objectives or rationales for longitudinal (or more specifically, in their case, prospective panel) research: (1) direct identification of intraindividual change, that is, whether individuals change from one period to another; (2) direct identification of interindividual similarities or differences in intraindividual change, that is, whether individuals change in the same or different ways; (3) analysis of interrelationships in behavioral change, that is, whether certain changes are correlated with each other; (4) analysis of causes or determinants of intraindividual change, that is, why individuals change from one period to another; and (5) analysis of causes or determinants of interindividual similarities or differences in intraindividual change, that is, why different individuals change in different ways from one period to another. All these objectives are concerned with patterns of developmental change, specifically at the individual level, although they are easily extended to aggregate levels (groups, organizations, cities, nations). At the individual level, intraindividual changes may include things people think (becoming more politically conservative), things they do (becoming employed, changing jobs, retiring), or things that are done to them (being arrested or being robbed). In the study of intraindividual change, age serves as a proxy for age-related physiological changes and exposure to social influences (Hobcraft et al., 1982) that may be difficult or costly to measure directly.

For some purposes, it may be reasonable to draw simple inferences about intraindividual change from cross-sectional data. For example, from cross-sectional data on rates of arrest and childbearing by age, we may reasonably infer that one's likelihood of being arrested or of having a baby is practically nonexistent before age 7, increases in adolescence and early adulthood, and diminishes substantially after age 65. There would seem to be little chance that these age-related differences may be explained by period effects or cohort characteristics. On the other hand, it would not be safe to infer that people become more conservative and less educated as they get older, based on cross-sectional data. As noted earlier, age differences in political attitudes at a particular period may reflect either changes in attitudes with age or constancy in attitudes over the life cycle coupled with differences in attitudes between cohorts. If older people have less education than younger people, it is not because they become "de-educated"; a more plausible explanation is that educational attainment has increased over time (a period effect), resulting in differences in the average educational level of successive cohorts.

The use of cross-sectional data to study the relationship between age and behavior amounts to the construction of a synthetic cohort, a practice common in the demographic study of mortality and fertility. Life expectancy and period total fertility rates, for example, are based on the use of cross-sectional mortality and fertility rates but are extrapolated by insurance companies (in the case of life expectancy) and others to describe what may happen to an individual or a cohort of individuals as they grow older. As Shryock and Siegel (1976:324) caution, the utility of synthetic cohort measures depends on the extent to which they reflect the actual experience of real cohorts (something that can be evaluated only with longitudinal research on cohorts). In some cases, cross-sectional and longitudinal data may lead to very different conclusions about developmental patterns. For example, Greenberg (1985), using officially reported crime, and Menard and Elliott (1990a), using self-reported delinquency, both found that cross-sectional and longitudinal data may produce different conclusions about the precise relationship between age and illegal behavior. In part, the differences between the longitudinal and cross-sectional results may be attributable to cohort size effects (Elliott et al., 1989:107-109; Menard & Elliott, 1990b).

A more compelling need for longitudinal data arises if we wish to study "career" patterns of behavior. The most obvious application of this is in the study of labor market careers, from initial job entry through patterns of promotion, job change, job loss, and eventually, either retirement or death. Closely related to this is the study of status attainment careers, which includes consideration of educational attainment as well as occupational status and income (e.g., Blau & Duncan, 1966). Other applications of the "career" perspective include marital histories (e.g., Becker et al., 1977), educational attainment and the process of learning (e.g., Heyns, 1978), and criminal careers (e.g., Blumstein et al., 1986). Such studies have in common a concern with patterns of entry, continuity, and exit from the behavior on which the career is based, and with the correlates and potential causes associated with changes or discontinuities in the behavior (unemployment and obtaining a new job, divorce and remarriage, dropout and reentry in education, suspension and resumption of criminal behavior). Only with longitudinal data, and more specifically, panel data, can many of the questions regarding developmental career patterns be answered.

Life course research (Giele & Elder, 1998) is similar to the study of individual careers but broadens the career paradigm to explicitly locate intraindividual change within a broader historical and social context. Integral to the life course perspective are issues of (1) location in time (history) and place (society and culture); (2) linked lives—the integration of individuals' lives with one another at the interpersonal and social institutional levels; (3) human agency—the ability and tendency of individuals to set goals and decide how to pursue them; and (4) timing of lives—individuals making decisions about whether and when to act in certain ways or formulating strategies for living based not only on internalized goals but also in response to external events or conditions. In contrast to perspectives that see life transitions as progressing through a fixed sequence of stages, the life course perspective recognizes the interindividual variation in the sequencing of life transitions as responses to differences in individual goals (human agency) and external influences (timing of lives). Life course research focuses on phenomena that can be adequately analyzed only with long-term longitudinal research: event histories or trajectories that differ across individuals in timing, duration, or rates of change.

Longitudinal data are also important in experimental research and evaluation research. Most experimental designs and quasi-experimental designs are inherently longitudinal, with measurement occurring both before (pretest) and after (posttest) the experimental treatment or intervention is administered (Campbell & Stanley, 1963), in order to ascertain whether differences at the posttest are attributable to the treatment or to preexisting differences between treatment and control groups. In experimental designs, even when a pretest is not used, the researcher assumes that the randomization of the assignment of subjects to different treatments produces groups that either do not differ on any important variable or whose deviations from equality are subject to known statistical distributions. Even a posttest-only experimental design thus includes a critical longitudinal assumption, namely, that a difference between the experimental and control groups at the posttest represents a change from the pretest, at which it is assumed, without possibility of proof or disproof, that there is little or no difference between the experimental and the control groups. Similarly, pretest or base-line data are often collected in evaluation research (Rossi et al., 1999). The absence of pretest or baseline data has the effect of rendering uncertain whether differences after some treatment or intervention may be wholly attributable to the treatment or intervention, or to preexisting differences between the group that did and the group that did not receive the treatment or intervention.

Developmental Trends in Relationships Among Variables. Parallel to the earlier concern with examining changes in the strength or pattern of rela-tionships from one period to another, we may want to examine changes in the strength or pattern of relationships from one age to another. Here again, the issue of whether to base the comparison on cross-sectional (intercohort) or longitudinal (intracohort) data may arise, and as before, the decision hinges on whether we are concerned with how well the developmental changes are reflected in the cross-sectional data. If longitudinal data are used, the issue of whether any change that occurs is attributable to age, period, or cohort effects must again be considered.

In a study of 341 adolescent boys in New Jersey, LaGrange and White (1985) found that for older (age 18) and younger (age 12) adolescent boys, only one variable, the extent of association with delinquent friends, had a substantial effect on delinquent behavior. For 15-year-old boys, however, family and school variables also affected delinquent behavior, sometimes more than association with delinquent friends. Although their sample size was small, and the age-specific subsamples were even smaller (81 to 138 cases for the three separate age groups), their study raises the important point that the results of multivariate causal analysis may vary, at least with regard to the strength of relationships, depending on the age of the respon-dents in the sample. Because their data are cross-sectional (different age groups measured in the same year), it is not possible to rule out another potential explanation: The differences may not be age specific but may be cohort specific instead. Full resolution of this issue would require a repli-cation, preferably with longitudinal data.

Using data from the National Youth Survey, a prospective longitudinal panel survey of respondents aged 11 to 17 in 1976 and 21 to 27 in 1986, Menard et al. (1989) found that marriage during adolescence was positively associated with substance use and mental health problems but that marriage during young adulthood (ages 21-27) was negatively associated with substance use and mental health problems. Being enrolled in school had a negative association with illegal behavior, substance use, and mental health problems in adolescence but no association with illegal behavior, substance use, or mental health problems for young adults. Wofford (1989), analyzing the same sample, found that employment was associated with higher rates of serious illegal behavior in adolescence and lower rates of serious illegal behavior in young adulthood (ages 18-24 in this study). Substantively, these results require explanation. From a life course perspective, there may be age-specific norms for certain behaviors (school, marriage, work), and violating those norms may place one at greater risk of involvement in illegal or problem behavior. Methodologically, these results suggest that relationships among variables may change over the life course and that it may be appropriate to test for the existence of such changes. With cross-sectional data, such differences may be attributed to age or to intercohort differences; with longitudinal data on multiple cohorts, it becomes possible to estimate the extent to which the differences are developmental, as opposed to period or intercohort differences.

Causal Relationships[2]

Three criteria are essential to establish the existence of a causal relationship between any pair of variables (Asher, 1983; Babbie, 2001:75-76; Baltes & Nesselroade, 1979, p. 35; Blalock, 1964): (1) the phenomena or variables in question must covary, as indicated, for example, by differences between experimental and control groups or by a nonzero correlation between the two variables; (2) the relationship must not be attributable to any other variable or set of variables, that is, it must not be *spurious*, but must persist even when other variables are controlled, as indicated, for example, by successful randomization in an experimental design (no differences between experimental and control groups prior to treatment) or by a nonzero partial correlation between two variables with other variables held constant; and (3) the supposed cause must precede or be simultaneous with the supposed effect in time, as indicated by the change in the cause occurring no later than the associated change in the effect.[3] Evidence for the first two criteria may be obtained from purely cross-sectional or time-ordered cross-sectional data. The third criterion can usually be tested adequately only with longitudinal data. One exception is if biological or genetic characteristics (sex, race) are among the variables thought to produce an effect. With such variables, we may safely assume temporal order without longitudinal data because, in effect, whenever a fixed trait is suggested as a cause of a variable characteristic (political attitudes, illegal behavior), we have data that are at least partially time ordered; we know that the fixed trait must have occurred first. Put another way, the measurement of fixed biological or genetic characteristics may be made *at* a particular period, but it is *for all* periods, beginning at birth.

The situation becomes more complex if there is a possibility of a *non-recursive* causal relationship. In some theories, causal influences flow not only from *X* to *Y* but from *Y* to *X* as well. For example, Malthus (Appleman, 1976) hypothesized that (a) increased food supply per capita leads to increased fertility and (b) increased fertility leads to decreased food supply per capita. With only cross-sectional data, issues of causal order or direction regarding bivariate relationships cannot be resolved without agreement a priori on the elimination of causal relationships in certain directions (Blalock, 1962; Heise, 1975; Simon, 1954). Where there is a nonrecursive causal pattern involving a negative feedback loop, as suggested in Malthusian theory (above), it may be difficult to adequately model the process with only cross-sectional data, even using two-stage least squares (e.g., Berry, 1984), structural equation modeling (Bollen, 1989; Hayduk, 1987; Kaplan, 2000), or other fairly sophisticated methods of data analysis. With longitudinal panel data (repeated cross-sectional data may not be adequate here), it becomes more likely that the issues of causal order can be resolved and that tests for causal influences in both directions can be made. (It is more probable, but not logically guaranteed, that longitudinal data will permit reliable estimates of reciprocal effects; for example, measurement periods may not be precise enough to separate the occurrence of changes in one variable from the occurrence of changes in another and thus to resolve the issue of indeterminate ordering.) In the example of Malthusian theory, with its negative feedback loop, fairly long time series data may be required for an adequate test of the theory.

Stage-State Analysis of Temporal and Causal Order for Qualitative Variables. In some cases, it may be possible to identify a distinct "start" for two variables and to ascertain the true temporal order between the two. In such cases, one cannot necessarily infer that the first variable to change causes the second (the criteria of covariation and nonspuriousness must still be met), but such a test would provide evidence that the second variable to change did not cause the first. When variables can be coded to indicate whether a presumed causal variable or a presumed dependent (effect) variable has changed, stage-state analysis may be used to indicate the temporal order of those changes. These changes may be measured as simple dichotomies (yes, change has occurred, or no, change has not occurred). One important type of change is the onset or initiation of a particular state or type of behavior. This refers to the first time that a case enters a particular state or, correspondingly, the first time that an individual engages in a particular type of behavior. Other possible changes include escalation of behavior (entry of a higher state on an ordinal scale), de-escalation or reduction (entry of a lower state on an ordinal scale), and suspension of behavior (permanent or temporary exit from all states that indicate involvement in a particular kind of behavior).

Three hypotheses suggested by criminologists have been that (a) drug use leads to other types of illegal behavior, (b) other types of illegal behavior lead to drug use, and (c) both drug use and crime are effects of the same set of causes (e.g., weak beliefs in conventional morality, involvement with delinquent or criminal friends). Huizinga et al. (1989) coded each behavior so that in each period, each respondent was classified as either *never* having initiated that behavior or as *ever* (even if not currently active) having initiated that behavior. Ever having initiated one behavior, coupled at some time with never having initiated the other, was counted as a case in which the one behavior was temporally prior to the other. Huizinga et al. found that the onset of drug use (including alcohol use) typically followed the onset of other types of illegal behavior (evidence against the hypothesis that drug use, at least initially, leads to other types of crime). For those individuals for whom temporal order of initiation was ascertainable (excluding respondents who had initiated both behaviors before the beginning of the study or who had initiated both within the same year), *all* respondents who ever became involved in both illegal behavior (excluding alcohol, marijuana, and hard drug use) and alcohol use became involved in illegal behavior first; *all* those who ever became involved in both illegal behavior and marijuana use became involved in illegal behavior first; and *all* those who ever became involved in both illegal behavior and hard drug use became involved in illegal behavior first. If a cause must precede an effect in time, then the onset of alcohol and drug use is largely ruled out as a cause of the onset of illegal behavior. The most plausible conclusions would be either that illegal behavior causes alcohol and drug use or that illegal behavior and drug use have common causes (i.e., the relationship is spurious), and illegal behavior tends to occur before alcohol or drug use as a result of these causes. Based on evidence in Elliott and colleagues (Elliot et al., 1985; Elliot et al., 1989), the latter explanation (spurious relationship) appears more likely. In a related study, Menard and Elliott (1990a) tested two theories, one of which suggested that involvement with delinquent friends leads to delinquent behavior and the other of which suggested that delinquent behavior leads to involvement with delinquent friends. They found that onset of association with delinquent friends typically preceded the onset of a respondent's own involvement in delinquent behavior, thus indicating support for the first theory (learning theory) and evidence against the second (control theory). Again, the establishment of temporal order is not in itself sufficient to establish causality, but it does provide evidence of the plausibility of one causal relationship as opposed to another.

Stage-state analysis may not always be a feasible approach to the examination of temporal or causal order. In some instances, the process or relationship being investigated has been ongoing for a long time, and it is not possible to collect data on onset. This is a problem of *left-hand censoring*, the failure to detect when a change has occurred because it happened before the first period for which data were collected. Alternatively, the variables being analyzed may have no meaningful onset or suspension. In cross-national models, for example, no nation ever has "zero" economic production or "zero" mortality or fertility at any period in its existence. These are characteristics of a nation that persist through time, and one cannot establish causal or temporal order by asking which started first. Changes in both variables take place from one period to the next, and stage-state models cannot disentangle which is cause and which is effect.

Temporal Order of Measurement, Causal Order, and Linear Panel Analysis. When there is no meaningful "start" or onset that allows us to say that a change in one variable occurred before any change in another variable, simply measuring one variable for an earlier period and the other variable for a later period is not sufficient to establish the first as temporally or causally prior to the second, as explained in more detail under the heading "Not-Quite-Longitudinal Designs" in Chapter 3. This is particularly true when the analysis includes a mixture of point and interval measures of variables. A point measure is one that is obtained for a single point in time (e.g., the day on which the interview occurs). Attitudinal measures are typically point measures. An interval measure involves a count of events, or a frequency, measured for an extended interval of time (e.g., the year preceding the interview). Many measures of behavior, especially frequency (how many times) and time span (for how long a period) measures, are interval measures. (This should not be confused with interval scales, which are scales with certain measurement properties; interval measures are defined in terms of the amount of time over which the measurement is taken.) The fact that a point measure is asked only for a very short span of time (right now) and an interval measure is asked for a very long span of time (all of last year) does not mean that the point measure is valid only for the day on which it is measured or that the interval measure is valid for the entire year for which it is measured. It is entirely possible, for example, that moral beliefs measured on the day of the interview have been stable for the past 10 months (at which time they changed from stronger to weaker) and that marijuana use reported for the previous year all occurred within the past 8 months (prior to which there was no marijuana use by the respondent). Even though the times for which the measurements were taken might indicate that marijuana use changed before beliefs, the true temporal (and causal, if other conditions are met) order in this example would be that the change in belief preceded the change in marijuana use.

One approach to identifying causal direction that can help disentangle causal order in studies that involve variables for which there is no meaningful beginning or ending (and which are therefore not amenable to stage-state analysis) is linear panel analysis (Finkel, 1995; Kessler & Greenberg, 1981). In linear panel analysis, any variables between which we are trying to ascertain causal order are treated as dependent (*endogenous*) variables and are measured for at least two periods (*waves*). The time between the periods for which the variables are measured is called the *measurement interval* (not to be confused with interval scales or interval measures; for the latter, see the preceding paragraph). There may or may not also be variables in the model that are treated only as predictors or independent (*exogenous*) variables, measured only once for a period at the same time as or before the first wave for which the endogenous variables are first measured. Regardless of whether there are other predictors, at least one prior value of each endogenous variable (a *lagged endogenous variable*) can be included as a possible predictor of the most recent value of that same variable. The inclusion of a lagged endogenous variable in the equation helps control for effects of unmeasured variables and provides a relatively conservative test for the existence of a nonspurious, nonzero causal relationship.

The linear panel model may include either or both of *lagged* and *instantaneous* effects. If the time it takes for the impact of one variable on the other is about as long as or longer than the measurement interval, the effect will appear to be lagged, possibly by more than one measurement interval. If the time it takes for the impact of one variable on another is much shorter than the measurement interval, the effect will appear to be instantaneous. For both linear panel and stage-state models, if the change in both variables occurs in the same period, it is possible that the measurement interval is too long and reducing the length of the measurement interval would allow us to separate the two changes. If the specified lag is too short, however, a strong relationship may appear to be weak because the full impact of changes in the independent variable have not yet been reflected in the dependent variable. Whenever the measurement interval (or some integral multiple thereof) does not correspond closely to the length of time it takes the independent variable to have its full effect on the dependent variable, there is a danger of incorrect causal inferences or, even more likely, underestimation of the effect of the independent variable on the dependent variable.

A two-variable, three-wave panel model is illustrated in Figure 2.1. The two variables are X and Y, and their subscripts refer to the time or wave of the panel for which they were measured. In Figure 2.1, the arrows indicate

20

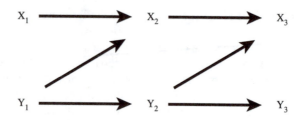

Figure 2.1. Hypothetical Causal Relationship Between X and Y.

that the most recent value of X is influenced by the next most recent value (arrows from X_1 to X_2 and from X_2 to X_3), but not by earlier values (no arrow directly from X_1 to X_3). The same pattern applies to Y. In addition, there is a lagged effect from Y to X (arrows from Y_1 to X_2 and from Y_2 to X_3), which indicates that Y causes X. The absence of any arrows from X to Y indicates that X does not cause Y, and Figure 2.1 also indicates that there are no instantaneous effects (no arrows directly between X_1 and Y_1, X_2 and Y_2, X_3 and Y_3).

Menard and Elliott (1994) used linear panel analysis to test for recipro-cal effects among delinquent behavior, attitudes toward delinquent behav-ior, and involvement with friends who were engaged in delinquent behavior. Using a three-wave model, with earlier behavior, attitudes, and patterns of association included as possible influences on later behavior, attitudes, and patterns of association, and examining both recursive (no simultaneous reciprocal effects) and nonrecursive (including simultaneous reciprocal effects) models, they found evidence for a simultaneous recipro-cal effect between behavior and patterns of association. They also found that (1) attitudes influenced patterns of association, but not quite as strongly as patterns of association influenced attitudes; (2) attitudes and behavior influenced one another, but only weakly; and (3) patterns of association influenced behavior more strongly than behavior influenced patterns of association. This last finding mirrors the finding described earlier (Menard & Elliott, 1990a) for the onset of delinquent behavior and association with delinquent friends, but here we are concerned with the annual frequency of delinquent behavior, not with its onset. As illustrated by this example, if both stage-state and linear panel analyses are possible, the results may be complementary and may help uncover complex interactive or reciprocal relationships that would be undiscovered without a thorough analysis of causal order. When there are strong theoretical reasons for believing that a certain causal relationship exists, one test of the theory is to verify the existence of the hypothesized temporal or causal order. When competing theories posit different and conflicting causal orderings, analysis of temporal or causal order may provide a strong test (Platt, 1964) of competing theories.

Granger Causality. Another approach that tests for both causal direction and strength of causal influence was proposed by Granger (1969; see also Cromwell et al., 1994). For two variables X_t and Y_t, both of which can be expressed as stationary time series (see "Time Series Analysis" in Chapter 5) with zero means,

$$X_t = \sum_{j=1}^{m} a_j X_{t-j} + \sum_{j=1}^{m} b_j Y_{t-j} + e_t$$

and

$$Y_t = \sum_{j=1}^{m} c_j X_{t-j} + \sum_{j=1}^{m} d_j Y_{t-j} + f_t$$

where e_t and f_t are taken to be two uncorrelated white noise series, and m is greater than zero but less than the length of the time series. According to the criterion of Granger causality, Y causes X if some b_j does not equal zero (implicitly, b_j must be statistically significantly different from zero). Correspondingly, X causes Y if some c_j is not equal to zero. In effect, the question posed by the test for Granger causality becomes, "Is there variation in one variable that cannot be explained by past values of that variable but that can be explained by past values of another variable?" If the answer is yes, then the second variable "Granger-causes" the first. Notice that if $m = 1$, and if there are only two periods in the series, the test for Granger causality reduces to a test for the statistical significance of the coefficients of exogenous variables (all measured at time 1) on the endogenous variable (measured at time 2) when the lagged endogenous variable (measured at time 1) is included in the equation. In other words, Y_2 is modeled as a function of Y_1 and X_1 (and there may be more than one X variable measured at time 1). Instantaneous effects (e.g., from X_2 to Y_2) are excluded from the model. In a longitudinal panel sample, this amounts to a two-wave linear panel model with no instantaneous effects.

The choice of m is arbitrary within the limits imposed by the length of the time series. Barnard and Krautmann (1988) used a single lagged endogenous variable (Y_{t-1}) with X measured at three periods (X_{t-1}, X_{t-2}, and X_{t-3}). Sims (1972) used lags of length 8 and also used "future lags" (in effect allowing future values of Y to influence the current value of Y). To be a cause of Y in Sims's model, X must explain variation in Y that is unexplained by both past and future values of Y. Wright (1989) separately analyzed lags of 1, 2, 3, 4, and 5 for the endogenous variable. There is some inconsistency in the results for different lags when this approach is taken. For example, Granger causality may be confirmed at lags of 3 and 4, but not at lags of 1, 2, or 5. How are we to interpret such results?

In general, the more prior that values of the endogenous variable are in the equation, the greater is the likelihood of rejecting the hypothesis of Granger causality, but the inclusion of additional values of the endogenous variable may have no significant effect beyond some number. This number may be estimated by modeling the endogenous variable as an autoregressive time series or by calculating separate ordinary least squares regression models and examining the change in the explained variance (R^2) produced by the inclusion of each additional lagged endogenous variable (e.g., by the addition of Y_{t-4}). If there is no statistically significant change in the explained variance (see, e.g., the test suggested in Agresti & Finlay, 1997), there would seem to be little point in including this term in the equation. It may well be that a lag of 1 is sufficient both to explain the variance in the dependent variable and to reject the hypothesis of Granger causality. If so, there may be little point in proceeding beyond lag 1. It is possible that X_t and Y_t will not be stationary time series. For short time series (e.g., five or fewer periods), this is unlikely to matter a great deal. For very long series (e.g., 100 or more periods), it should be possible to test for stationarity. For series of moderate length (e.g., 20-40 periods), it may not be possible to determine whether the conditions for applying the Granger test have been met. There seem to be ample possibilities for misusing the test, and the assumption of stationarity should not be taken for granted. Caution should be taken, particularly when applying the test to series too short for analysis using Autoregressive Integrated Moving Average (ARIMA) time series methods, to be discussed in more detail in Chapter 5.

Other Issues in Causal Analysis. In addition to addressing issues of causal order and the existence of reciprocal effects, longitudinal data and analysis in conjunction with causal modeling may be used to examine the distinction between long- and short-term effects on behavior. McCord (1983) found long-term consequences on adult aggression and antisocial behavior of childhood aggressiveness, parental aggressiveness, parental control, and parental affection. Studies of the Perry Preschool Project (Berrueta-Clement et al., 1984; Schweinhart & Weikart, 1980; Weikart et al., 1978), a Head Start-type preschool program, found short-term effects on student behavior and learning that seemed to dissipate in later years, then reemerge as long-term effects as the students entered adolescence. With methods such as event history analysis (e.g., Blossfeld et al., 1989), it becomes easier, given appropriate data, to directly combine the analysis of age and period effects with causal analysis to explain developmental and historical change. These examples fall under the broader headings of describing change and of causal analysis, yet they indicate that questions about change and causality may sometimes be more complex (long- vs. short-term change, causal influences on rates of change) than simple questions of whether and why changes occur. The type of question that is asked may have important implications for which of several possible longitudinal designs is most appropriate for a particular study.

Serendipity and Intentionality in Longitudinal Data

The earliest longitudinal data in the social sciences, national census data, were probably not originally collected for the purposes of measuring change or of establishing the direction or magnitude of causal relationships. More typically, the two purposes of early censuses were conscription and taxation (Thomlinson, 1976). Later, in the United States, political apportionment was the only constitutionally mandated purpose of the census, and in more recent years the census has also been used as a basis for allocating funds from the federal government to the states. The fact that census data may be used to measure change and perhaps to infer the nature of causal relationships has been, at least until recently, more serendipitous than intentional. The same may be said about many other sources of longitudinal data as well. In the 20th century, and especially since World War II, the collection of longitudinal data for the analysis of change and causality has become more conscious and deliberate, as social science research generally, and longitudinal research in particular, have come to be more highly valued by governments and by the scientific community. Still, it remains the case that longitudinal research is a secondary, not primary, reason for the collection of much periodic data by government agencies. As a result, methods of collecting data or definitions of variables may change in ways that render data less than fully comparable from one period to another.

In demography, for example, the United Nations has attempted to set standards for the counting of infant deaths and the calculation of infant mortality rates. Aside from problems of cross-national standardization, the adoption of those standards by countries such as Sweden in 1960 and Spain in 1975 (Hartford, 1984) produced discontinuities in the data so that comparisons of infant mortality rates over certain time periods, for example, from 1970 to 1980 in Spain, are imprecise and problematic. Completeness of registration or counting of events may also vary over time, again making even crude measurements of change problematic. The President's Commission on Law Enforcement and the Administration of Justice (1967)

24

cautioned that problems in coverage of rural areas in the United States rendered the crime statistics reported by the Federal Bureau of Investigation (annual) prior to 1958 "neither fully compatible with nor nearly so reliable" as data reported for subsequent years. Issues such as these may be more adequately addressed when data are collected primarily for longitudinal research to begin with, but it is worth cautioning that data that are initially collected for other purposes, and to which researchers serendipitously have access, should be carefully scrutinized to determine their suitability for the purposes of longitudinal research. Changes in how units or events are defined and counted or in the extent to which the intended universe of cases is adequately sampled may render some data sets unsuitable for use in longitudinal research.

3. DESIGNS FOR LONGITUDINAL DATA COLLECTION

Not-Quite-Longitudinal Designs

In Chapter 1, longitudinal research was contrasted with pure cross-sectional research, in which data are collected only once, contemporaneously, for each variable for each case. Prospective panel, retrospective panel, and repeated cross-sectional designs were described. Some studies do not fall neatly under the definition of longitudinal research or of pure cross-sectional research. Ahluwalia (1974, 1976) used data on per capita gross national product and income inequality to examine the relationship between income inequality and economic development. Because data on income inequality were collected sporadically, Ahluwalia used data in which for each case, income inequality and per capita gross national product were measured at the same time, but for different countries (cases) measurement occurred in different years (e.g., for one country the two variables would be measured for the year 1955, and for another country the two variables would be measured for the year 1972). By performing a single, cross-sectional analysis on data collected over an 18-year span (1955-1972), Ahluwalia's analysis implicitly assumed that the 18 years constituted a single period. Equivalently, this approach assumed that the data on both per capita gross national product and income inequality were stable (no major changes in values, or at least in the ranking, of countries on these variables), or at least that the relationship between these variables remained largely unchanged over this 18-year time span. Such an assumption should be made only after careful consideration and preferably with empirical support as well. Contrary to the assumption of stability, Menard (1983, 1986) presented evidence of instability in income inequality over time, to the point that for the period included in Ahluwalia's data, the ranking of countries with respect to income inequality changed. At the same time, per capita gross national product remained stable. In effect, Ahluwalia's data may represent a series of cross-sections in which the same variables are measured repeatedly, but the cases are neither comparable nor identical from one period to the next. The period used is so long that there is reason to doubt that the measurements for all of the cases could properly be considered contemporaneous.

In a somewhat different vein, Tolnay and Christenson (1984) deliberately selected variables that were measured at different times for use in a causal path analysis of fertility, family planning, and development. Each variable was measured at the same time for all countries, but different variables were measured at different times, in order to match the temporal order of measurement with the causal order in the path model. This is just the opposite of the pattern in Ahluwalia's data. For Ahluwalia, variables are measured at the same time for each case, but cases are measured at different times; for Tolnay and Christenson, cases are measured at the same time for each variable, but variables are measured at different times. Although measurement occurred at different times for different variables, each variable is measured only once for each case, and the data cannot be used to perform even the simplest true longitudinal analysis (e.g., measuring change in a variable from one period to another). The analysis used by Tolnay and Christenson is essentially cross-sectional in nature. Had they chosen to postulate instantaneous effects, the analysis could have been performed just as well with purely cross-sectional data. For the purposes of their analysis (evaluating direct and indirect effects of family planning effort and development on fertility), this design is appropriate, and may have an advantage over models in which causal order in the path model and temporal order of measurement are not the same (Menard & Elliott, 1990a). The design used by Tolnay and Christenson, with time-ordered data and cross-sectional analysis, may be described as a *time-ordered cross-sectional design*. Although it is not truly a longitudinal design, by the definition presented earlier, it may have some advantages over a pure cross-sectional design for purposes of causal analysis.

The use of time-ordered cross-sectional data, as in Tolnay and Christenson (1984), is desirable once temporal order has been established, but it is insufficient to ensure that one does not "predict" a cause from its effect. Suppose, for example, that the true causal relationship between two variables, X and Y, is the relationship diagrammed in Figure 2.1. Prior values of X influence subsequent values of X; prior values of Y influence subsequent values of Y; and prior values of Y influence subsequent values of X, that is, Y is a cause of the effect X with some finite time lag. Suppose, however, that we mistakenly believe X to be a cause of Y, and in a time-ordered cross-sectional design, we include X_2 as a cause of Y_3, excluding all other X (X_1 and X_3) and Y (Y_1 and Y_2). Despite the fact that we have the wrong causal order, we will probably discover a relationship between X_2 and Y_3, if only because X_2 is directly affected by Y_1 and Y_3 is indirectly (via Y_2) influenced by Y_1. In other words, there is a spurious relationship between X_2 and Y_3. If the variables change relatively slowly over time (i.e., if they are relatively stable), then similar correlations will be obtained whether we compare X_2 and Y_3, X_3 and Y_2, or some purely cross-sectional combination (e.g., X_2 and Y_2) of the two variables. With a true longitudinal design (e.g., a prospective panel design) and analysis, it might be possible to ascertain the true causal direction in the relationship between X and Y. With cross-sectional data, even time-ordered cross-sectional data, we run the risk of undetectable misspecification because of incorrect causal ordering in the model being estimated. With longitudinal data, incorrect causal ordering is more likely to be detected, for example by stage-state analysis or linear panel analysis of temporal or causal order, and the model can be corrected.

Total Population Designs

Figure 3.1 represents four types of longitudinal designs. In Figure 3.1, the horizontal dimension represents the period (a month, year, or decade) for which data are collected, and the vertical dimension represents the cases (population or sample) for which data are collected. In a *total population design*, the total population is surveyed or measured in each period of the study. Because some individuals die and others are born from one period to the next, the cases are not identical from one period to the next, but if the periods are short, the overwhelming majority of cases may be the same from one period to the next. As one example, the decennial census of the United States attempts to collect data on age, sex, ethnicity, and residence of the total population of the United States every 10 years and does so with an accuracy estimated at 95-99% (Armas, 2001; Hogan & Robinson, 2000; Robey, 1989). With somewhat lower, but still substantial accuracy and completeness of coverage, the Federal Bureau of Investigation's *Uniform Crime Reports* attempt to collect data on arrests for specific offenses and, for a limited set of offenses, crimes known to the police, and the age, sex, race, and residence (urban, suburban, or rural) of arrestees for all police jurisdictions in the United States.

As with any data collection effort, the total population design may have problems of missing cases or measurement error. Because the total

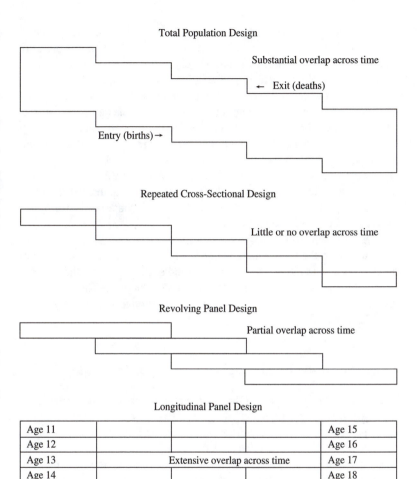

Figure 3.1. Longitudinal Designs for Data Collection

population is included, the design should be appropriate for measuring or inferring period trends, but close examination of age and cohort effects (as discussed earlier) may be necessary to clarify the nature of those trends. For example, apparent changes in the number or rate of arrests may reflect changes in population composition (percentage in the arrest-prone adolescent ages) rather than changes in individual or group behavior (Chilton & Spielberger, 1971). Separation of age, period, and cohort effects is thus as much an issue for the total population design as for any other design, but the design poses no special problems in this regard. Developmental changes may be examined both cross-sectionally (within a given year, across cohorts) and longitudinally (within a given cohort, across years, if there are enough periods to examine the developmental change in question), and the results of the two approaches for evaluating developmental effects may be compared. With proper selection of appropriate periods, cohorts, or other subpopulations, any type of longitudinal analysis may be performed on data collected in a total population design, again with the qualification that there are enough separate periods to permit use of a particular method. For example, linear panel analysis typically requires only 2 or 3 periods (Finkel, 1995; Kessler & Greenberg, 1981), but ARIMA time series models ideally involve a minimum of 50 distinct periods (Box & Jenkins, 1970, p. 18) and may require 100 to 250 periods to provide adequate power for model testing (Yaffee & McGee, 2000).

Each of the other three longitudinal designs in Figure 3.1 involves a sample drawn from the total population and is thus a subset of the total population design. The three designs differ in the extent to which the same or comparable cases are studied from one period to the next. This distinction has important implications for which types of longitudinal analysis are possible with each design.

Repeated Cross-Sectional Designs

In the repeated cross-sectional design, the researcher typically draws independent probability samples at each measurement period. These samples will typically contain entirely different sets of cases for each period, or the overlap will be so small as to be considered negligible, but the cases should be as comparable from one period to another as would be the case in a total population design. An example of the repeated cross-sectional design is the National Survey of Youth, conducted by Martin Gold and his associates (Gold & Reimer, 1975; Williams & Gold, 1972). Gold and his associates collected data on two separate national probability samples of youth, one in 1967 and one in 1972. From these samples, they were able to infer that despite changes in arrest rates of juveniles from 1967 to 1972, there was little actual change in self-reported delinquent behavior from 1967 to 1972. Johnston et al. (annual) have collected data on national probability samples of high school seniors since 1975 in the Monitoring the Future study. Their repeated cross-sectional data, like the data collected by Gold and his associates, permit the examination of trends in attitudes and behaviors within a specific age group over time. The World Values Surveys (Inglehart, 1997) have been used to examine the relationships among long-term changes in attitudes and beliefs, economic development, and political culture. Other examples of repeated cross-sectional designs include public opinion polls, election polls, and the General Social Survey, an annual general population survey conducted by the National Opinion Research Center, which covers a wide range of topics (including marriage and family, sexual behavior and sex roles, labor force participation, education, income, religion, politics, crime and violence, health, and personal happiness) and emphasizes exact replication of questions to permit comparisons across time (Davis & Smith, 1992).

The principal limitations to the repeated cross-sectional design are its inappropriateness for studying developmental patterns within cohorts and its inability to resolve issues of causal order. Both of these limitations result directly from the fact that in the repeated cross-sectional design, the same cases are not measured repeatedly or for multiple periods. Developmental patterns may be examined by looking at differences across ages (i.e., across cohorts) for each measurement period in which multiple cohorts are measured, but the only advantage of the repeated cross-sectional design over a pure cross-sectional design for this purpose is that the repeated cross-sectional design builds in the possibility of replicating cross-sectional results across periods. This reduces, but does not eliminate, the possibility that the developmental patterns suggested by intercohort comparisons may not reflect the developmental patterns indicated by intracohort comparisons. For causal order, the absence of data on the same cases for two or more periods means that stage-state analysis and linear panel analysis of temporal order are not possible (unless—and this is quite unlikely—an adequate procedure for matching different cases measured in different periods is available). The measurement of change in repeated cross-sectional designs can only be made at the aggregate level, for the sample or for subsamples (e.g., males and females, ethnic groups, social classes). It cannot be made at the level of individual cases. Limitations such as these have led many authors, particularly in developmental psychology (e.g., Baltes & Nesselroade, 1979), to argue that the repeated cross-sectional design should not really be considered a longitudinal design. Baltes et al. (1979) nonetheless consider the repeated cross-sectional design (which they describe as a cross-sectional sequence) in the study of cohort effects.

The repeated cross-sectional design is generally appropriate for measuring aggregate period trends. *If* causal order is already well established, and *if* the time lag between cause and effect can be assumed to be short relative to the interval between measurement periods, the repeated cross-sectional design may also be used for causal analysis in models that are essentially cross-sectional in nature. *If* intercohort and intracohort developmental differences closely reflect one another, there is no obstacle to the use of the repeated cross-sectional design with multiple cohorts for the analysis of developmental patterns, again in an essentially cross-sectional analysis. For both causal inference and developmental analysis, other types of longitudinal designs are needed to indicate whether a repeated cross-sectional design may reasonably be used. Finally, the repeated cross-sectional design permits the researcher to replicate cross-sectional results from one period to another. If, however, we are interested in intracohort developmental changes, or in ascertaining causal order, other longitudinal designs for data collection are preferable.

Revolving Panel Designs

Revolving panel designs collect data on a sample of cases either retrospectively or prospectively for some sequence of measurement periods, then drop some subjects and replace them with new subjects. The revolving panel design may reduce problems of panel mortality and repeated measurement in prospective studies (to be discussed in Chapter 4) or problems of extended recall periods in retrospective studies. Retention of a particular set of cases over several measurement periods allows short-term measurement of change on the individual or case level, short-term analysis of intracohort developmental change, and panel analysis. Replacement of the subsample that is dropped in a measurement period with a new but comparable subsample of cases permits analysis of long-term patterns of aggregate change. If the time lag between cause and effect is smaller than the time (periods) for which cases are retained in the sample, analysis of temporal and causal order is possible. The combination of longitudinal data involving repeated measurement on some cases with data that do not involve repeated measurement on others may permit comparisons that can indicate whether repeated measurement is producing any bias in the data (e.g., increased or decreased willingness to report events after either building up some level of trust or finding out that reporting leads to long and tedious follow-up questions).

The National Crime Survey,[4] funded by the Department of Justice and implemented by the U.S. Census Bureau, is a good example of a revolving panel design. Household members are periodically interviewed about criminal victimization of household members for seven offenses (rape, robbery, aggravated assault, simple assault, burglary, larceny, and motor vehicle theft). Households are selected for inclusion by probability sampling, interviewed seven times (at 6-month intervals) over a 3-year time span, then dropped from the sample and replaced by newly selected households. With the household as the unit of analysis, this permits analysis of short-term trends in rates of victimization within households and both short- and long-term trends in aggregate or average rates of victimization. Longer term developmental trends within households, however, cannot be analyzed.

The Kansas City police patrol experiment (Kelling et al., 1974) also used a revolving panel design to collect data on victimization. A sample of 1,200 households was used in the pretest; half of the households were retained and the other half replaced for the posttest. As a result it was possible to compare those who had been interviewed twice (pretest and posttest) with those who had been interviewed only once (posttest only) and to rule out the possibility that the results (no difference between control and experimental police beats) were a consequence of bias from repeated interviewing. The revolving panel design would also be appropriate for longitudinal research on individuals within a particular age range, such as adolescents or those over age 65, in order to prevent serious problems of sample attrition as respondents "age out" of adolescence or die in old age. The revolving sample for limited age ranges permits the researcher to maintain a sufficient number of cases (see, e.g., Kraemer & Thiemann, 1987) for complex analyses or analyses of small subsamples within the larger sample.

Longitudinal Panel Designs

In a longitudinal panel design, the same set of cases is used in each period. In practice, there may be some variation from one period to another as a result of missing data. For example, when cases are individuals, some of those individuals may die between one measurement period and the next, others may not agree to cooperate, and others may move to new locations and not be found by the researcher. All of these are sources of *panel attrition* and apply primarily to *prospective* panel designs, in which measurement or data collection occurs during more than one period. Panel attrition, as such, is not a problem for *retrospective* panel designs, in which data collection may occur only once, at one period, but in which data are collected for two or more periods (prior to or during the period in which the data are being collected). In retrospective panel designs, however, there may be sampling bias as a result of excluding respondents who have died by the last period for which the data are collected or from whom data would otherwise have been available for earlier periods but not for the last period. In both retrospective and prospective panel designs, missing data may result from failure of the respondent to remember past events, behaviors, or attitudes or from unwillingness by the respondent to divulge some information and also from inability of the researcher to locate or obtain cooperation from some respondents. In principle, there need be no difference in the quality of the data obtained in prospective and retrospective panel designs, but differences do occur in practice (as discussed in Chapter 4).

A longitudinal panel design that includes multiple cohorts (as illustrated in Figure 3.1) should permit any type of longitudinal analysis, if the numbers of periods and cohorts are sufficient. Single-cohort panel designs do not permit comparisons between cohorts, but multiple-cohort designs permit analysis of age, period, and cohort effects, descriptions of developmental and historical change, analysis of the temporal order of events, linear panel analysis, and causal analysis. As an example, the National Youth Survey, conducted by Delbert S. Elliott and his associates (Elliott et al., 1985; Elliot et al., 1989) selected a national probability sample of youths aged 11 to 17 (seven cohorts) in 1976 and has continued to reinterview this same sample periodically, most recently in 1993. Data from the National Youth Survey have been used (a) to estimate and analyze period trends in illegal behavior (Menard, 1987b); (b) to separate age, period, and cohort effects in drug use (Elliott et al., 1989; Menard & Huizinga, 1989) and illegal behavior (Elliott et al., 1989; Menard & Elliott, 1990b); (c) to test and replicate a theoretical model of illegal behavior in adolescence and young adulthood (Elliott et al., 1985; Elliott et al., 1989; Roitberg & Menard, 1995); (d) to demonstrate developmental changes in relationships between illegal behavior and predictors of illegal behavior (Menard et al., 1989; Wofford, 1989); (e) to examine continuity in illegal behavior from adolescence to adulthood (Menard & Mihalic, 2001); and (f) to ascertain the temporal order of variables in order to resolve contradictory claims by competing theories (Menard & Elliott, 1990a). These examples illustrate the breadth of analyses and results possible with multiple-cohort prospective panel data.

Other Variations

The designs diagrammed in Figure 3.1 are not the only possible designs for longitudinal research. It is possible, for example, to have a revolving sample in which subsamples may be dropped for one period, then re-included in the sample in a subsequent period. It is also possible to have a panel design in which cases are dropped, without replacement, after they meet some criterion (e.g., age 21). This latter design would result in a monotonically decreasing sample size that could pose problems for analysis of data from later years of the study (unless the design were further modified by replenishing the sample with new respondents from younger cohorts). The general considerations associated with the various designs for data collection do not change, however, with modifications of the four designs presented in Figure 3.1, and variations on these basic designs must be evaluated in terms of their adequacy for describing short- and long-term historical trends (period effects); describing intercohort and intracohort developmental changes (age effects); separating age, period, and cohort effects; and ascertaining not only the strength but also the direction (e.g., by stage-state analysis or linear panel analysis) of causal influences. Total population designs and longitudinal panel designs can be used for practically any type of longitudinal analysis, given a sufficient number of cohorts and measurement periods. Other designs are more limited, and their appropriateness must be judged in the context of a particular research problem.

With each of these designs, the number of cases and periods may vary, and as a result of this variation, different methods of analysis may be appropriate. If both the number of cases and the number of periods are large (e.g., several thousand cases and 100 or more periods), the possibilities for analysis are limited only by the quality of the data. If both the cases and periods are few in number (e.g., 1-10 cases over 2-10 periods), then any quantitative analysis may be problematic.[5] More characteristically, the number of cases may be fairly large (e.g., 1,000 cases at the individual level or 50 cases at the aggregate level) and the number of periods may be small (2-4), a situation for which linear panel analysis (Finkel, 1995; Kessler & Greenberg, 1981) is one appropriate method. Alternatively, the number of cases may be small (1-10) and the number of periods may be large (100 or more), a condition most amenable to time series analysis (Wei, 1990; Yaffee & McGee, 2000). The number of cases is in principle independent of the type of design. In a total population design, for example, at the individual level, the total population of a tribal society may number fewer than 100. In aggregate analysis, a cohort or a population, rather than its individual members, may be the unit of analysis, and the number of these aggregate units may be small. At the other end of the continuum, the revolving sample in the National Crime Survey includes more then 100,000 individuals from 60,000 households. All these possible combinations of type of design and number of cases are included within the broad category of longitudinal research. The different methods, and their applicability to different combinations of number of cases and number of periods, will be discussed further in Chapter 5.

4. ISSUES IN LONGITUDINAL RESEARCH

There is nothing unique about the methods used to collect data for longitudinal research. Longitudinal research, like cross-sectional research, relies upon three fundamental methods of gathering data: asking people questions, observing people's behavior, and observing the physical traces or results of people's behavior. Data may be collected for a single case, a small number of cases, or a very large number of cases; for everyone in a society, for a probability sample of people in a society, or for particular individuals who may or may not reflect either the society as a whole or some segment of society. Data may be kept and coded at the level of individuals or aggregated into households, census tracts, or nations. Periods for which data are collected may be short, consisting of a few hours, or long, consisting of several years. Standardized data collection instruments may be used, or data collection may be an interactive process that is unique to each case. Both longitudinal and cross-sectional research may involve case studies, ethnographies, experiments, sample surveys, censuses, or archival data collection. The one principal distinction between longitudinal and cross-sectional data collection, as noted earlier, is that in longitudinal research, data are collected on each variable for at least two periods.

The problems that arise regarding data quality in cross-sectional research thus arise in similar fashion for longitudinal research. Problems of internal and external measurement validity; measurement reliability; sampling; appropriateness of questions to the population being studied; adequacy of the randomization procedures in experimental designs; effects of interaction between subjects or respondents and experimenters, interviewers, or observers (in microsocial data collection); and issues of the relevance of the research (do we measure what is important or just what is easily measurable?) and research costs are as important in longitudinal research as they are in cross-sectional research. Some of these issues are even more problematic for longitudinal than for cross-sectional research. For example, biases in sampling may be amplified by repetition in repeated cross-sectional designs, or effects of researchers on respondents may be amplified by repeated contact between researchers and subjects in prospective panel designs. General discussions of these issues are available elsewhere (e.g., Babbie, 2001; Bickman & Rog, 1998). Here, we focus on issues and problems that are characteristic of longitudinal rather than cross-sectional designs.

Genesis Versus Prediction

Zazzo (1967, cited in Wall & Williams, 1970) argued that a distinction should be made between the study of the *genesis* of behavior and the study of the *prediction* of behavior. Prediction, according to Zazzo, is concerned with the stability of population characteristics over time and the extent to which external influences (changes in environment, therapeutic intervention) may modify those characteristics. Genesis, by contrast, focuses on stages or sequences of qualitative changes, with the goal of discovering laws of growth or developmental change. According to Zazzo, the study of the genesis of behavior may require the use of more qualitative methods: discarding large samples and predefined hypotheses and variables in favor of intensive study of a small number of cases, initially with no hypotheses about what variables are important, and discarding age (and chronological time) as a continuum along which change is measured in favor of measuring change with respect to prior states. Zazzo cited the work of Piaget (see, e.g., Piaget, 1948, 1951, 1952) as an example of research on genesis.

Without denying that the focus of most longitudinal research has been on prediction rather than genesis (as defined by Zazzo), we may nonetheless note that research on genesis has not been neglected at either the macrosocial or the microsocial level. At the macrosocial level, Rostow (1960) proposed a theory of stages of economic development, Black (1966) attempted to define stages of political development or political modernization, and the theory of the demographic transition, in its various incarnations (e.g., Caldwell, 1976; Davis, 1963; Notestein, 1945; Thompson, 1929) although not without its critics (Van de Walle & Knodel, 1980), has proven to be a durable perspective and a source for a great deal of research in demography (e.g., the aforementioned studies by Menard, 1987a; Tolnay & Christenson, 1984). At the microsocial level, Kandel and her associates (Kandel, 1975; Kandel & Faust, 1975; Kandel & Logan, 1984; Yamaguchi & Kandel, 1984a, 1984b) have examined the sequencing of stages of drug use and found evidence of progression from alcohol to marijuana to other illicit drugs, with few moving to a more advanced stage without first entering an earlier (less serious) one. Kandel's work has also demonstrated that research on genesis of behavior need not be isolated from predictive research. She and her associates have not only described sequences of progression in drug use but also have explained under what circumstances progression from one substance to another is most likely. To obtain a more complete account of patterns of development, then, we may study both the sequencing of behavior and the timing and correlates of progression from one stage to another.

Changes in Measurement Over Time

In 1930, Redfield (1930) published the results of his ethnographic study of a Mexican village, Tepoztlan, in which he described the village as harmonious and the people as well adjusted and content. Twenty-one years later, Lewis (1951) published his ethnographic study of the same village, and in contrast to Redfield, Lewis found considerable evidence of violence, cruelty, and conflict, both within the village and in its relationships with other villages (Gist & Fava, 1974:513). Fifty-five years after Mead (1928) published her ethnographic findings from Samoa, Freeman (1983) questioned and contradicted Mead's findings with his own ethnographic evidence from Samoa. Because of the differences in time, it is unclear whether the differences in findings reflect true changes or merely different biases or orientations on the part of the observers.

The problems so vividly illustrated by discrepant ethnographic studies may also arise in survey research. Martin (1983) described unsuccessful attempts to replicate surveys of victimization and surveys of confidence in American institutions in repeated cross-sectional survey designs. With regard to confidence in American institutions, nearly identical measures used by Harris polls and National Opinion Research Center studies produced not only different cross-sectional results but different trends as well. With regard to victimization, an Urban Institute study explicitly designed to replicate the standard procedures used by the Census Bureau in conducting the National Crime Survey (NCS) obtained victimization rates less than half those obtained for a comparable population in the NCS, conducted 1 year later, and lower also than the rates obtained in a telephone survey conducted at about the same time.

A second example of potential problems of changes in measurement also comes from the NCS. In 1992, the NCS changed the way it measured victimization, and its name was changed to the National Crime Victimization Survey (NCVS). The redesign resulted in higher estimated rates of criminal victimization. A cross-sectional comparison of the rates obtained by the NCS and NCVS in the first and second half, respectively, of 1992 was subsequently used to adjust data from the NCS to examine longer-term trends in victimization, but multiyear comparisons to examine trends in the two series were not performed. After the redesign, violent victimization peaked in 1994, then declined sharply, while property crime continued a decline that had been observed prior to the redesign (Rennison, 2000). Given the contrasting evidence from the violent and property victimization trends, it seems less plausible that changes in measurement are the explanation for the changes in violent victimization trends, but if we looked only at violent victimization, a reasonable argument could be made that the trends in victimization rates since 1992 reflected changes in measurement rather than changes in behavior.

Gold's (Gold & Reimer, 1975; Williams & Gold, 1972) repeated cross-sectional study of delinquent behavior appears to have been successful in replicating both the sampling procedures and the substantive results from the first wave to the second. One advantage to the surveys conducted by Gold and his associates was continuity with respect to the principal researcher. Without intimate knowledge of not only formal procedures but informal aspects of the research as well, it may be extremely difficult or impossible to completely replicate previous waves of data collection in a repeated cross-sectional or prospective (total population, revolving panel, longitudinal panel) longitudinal designs. The problem of standardization across periods or waves of data collection may be different for different data collection methods. Standardization across waves in survey research is aided by use of the same questionnaire from one wave of data to another, but variation in the way the questionnaire is administered by interviewers at different waves may still pose a problem; this is an issue, primarily, of interviewer training. For more qualitative research, the "instrument" for data collection may be the observer, and different observers may have different biases, focus on different aspects of the setting or behavior in the setting, and reach very different conclusions. Some researchers have suggested that the findings from participant observation studies may be inherently "idiosyncratic and difficult to replicate" (Blalock & Blalock, 1982:97).

Lack of standardization in data collection across time may arise for legitimate reasons. If a survey begins with adolescent respondents and follows them until they are in their late 20s or early 30s, questions about how favorably they view school may be important in the early years of the survey, and questions about how favorably they view their jobs or occupations may be more important later. Respondents will also be making transitions from families of orientation (parents and siblings) to families of procreation (spouses and children). If attitudes toward work or school, and family stress, are theoretically important predictors of some behavior (e.g., drug use), it may make sense to match the changes in respondents' lives with corresponding changes in the variables that are measured. Two questions are important here. First, can one variable measured at one stage of a respondent's life be equated with a conceptually similar variable (e.g., stress in family of orientation and stress in family of procreation) at a later stage? Second, is the transition abrupt or gradual? Do respondents undergo a period when involvement in both contexts is important (e.g., working and going to school at the same time), or is the change an abrupt one that involves completely leaving one context and immersing oneself in the other? By measuring the variables for both contexts at the same time, it is possible to directly estimate the relationship between the two variables and to see whether they have similar patterns of relationships with other variables. If the variables are highly correlated, and if they have the same pattern of relationships with other variables, a strong argument for concurrent validity (Bohrnstedt, 1983; Zeller & Carmines, 1980) may be established.

Other reasons for changes in instrumentation include new hypotheses, either from the study itself or from general advances in the relevant fields of social science, and changes in research staff and their respective interests

(Wall & Williams, 1970). The addition of new hypotheses to those with which the study began may also be a source of change. The dangers involved with each of these changes are readily apparent. If other studies have clearly discredited or refuted the hypotheses upon which the research project is based, it becomes practically meaningless to continue the research. The utter refutation of a theory or hypothesis is, however, exceedingly rare in the social sciences, and even then, the data may have some utility for replicating the refutation of the old hypothesis. Alternatively, shifting hypotheses, variables, and measurements part way through an ongoing longitudinal research project would mean that the two parts of the research, before and after the shift, might not be comparable. This potentially destroys the utility of the data, both before and after the shift, for the sort of longitudinal analysis that was originally intended. In addition, it runs the risk of having one's research dictated by what may later be recognized as a transient theoretical fashion.

Panel Attrition

In a longitudinal study of adolescent drug use, Newcomb and Bentler (1988) experienced a 55% attrition rate over an 8-year interval. Murray and Erickson (1987) reported an attrition rate of 50% in a study of marijuana use. Other studies have fared better. Clarridge et al. (1977) were able to achieve an attrition rate of 11% in a follow-up study of Wisconsin high school seniors 17 years after they were first interviewed. Dempster-McClain and Moen (1998) reported the results of a "catch-up" study of 427 mothers who had been interviewed at Cornell University in 1956 and who were subsequently interviewed 30 years later, in 1986. Of the 427 original respondents, 4% (19) could not be located, 19% (82) were deceased, 3% (13) refused to participate in the follow up, and 73% were successfully reinterviewed. Other prospective longitudinal panels such as the Panel Study of Income Dynamics (PSID) and the Survey of Income and Program Participation have reported retention rates (for those who responded in the first period of data collection) of 65-80% (Brown et al., 1996; Hill, 1992; Kalton et al., 1989). The National Youth Survey (NYS) (Elliott et al., 1989) reported an attrition rate less than 10% over a 5-year time span (with annual interviews), and 20% over a 17-year time span (when the interval between measurements had changed from 1 to 3 years). Combined with initial loss rates, however, attrition rates even from surveys with relatively high annual retention rates, such as the NYS or PSID, translate into total loss rates (percentages of respondents missing for at least one wave of data collection) over time of 40-50%, or total retention rates of 50-60%.

Insofar as respondents are lost in later waves of data collection, the measurement of change may be confounded because those respondents who are lost may differ from those who are retained in some systematic way (they may have had different average values on variables to begin with, or they may have changed in ways different from the rest of the sample). This is especially serious if losses come disproportionately from those with extreme values on the variables on which the research focuses, for example, the most frequent illicit drug users or the most serious criminals in studies of illegal behavior. It is thus not only the magnitude of the attrition but also the pattern of attrition with respect to critical variables in the study that may be problematic. This appears to be particularly relevant to studies of deviant or illegal behavior. For example, Walton et al. (1998) found that difficulty of recontact was related to involvement in substance use in a panel of substance abusers in treatment. Cordray and Polk (1983) found that even with relatively high attrition, respondents who remained over time in panels provided relatively accurate estimates of bivariate and multivariate relationships, but measures of prevalence and frequency of behavior were biased, particularly for general population samples. Thornberry et al. (1993) found that estimates of prevalence and frequency of delinquency and drug use would be biased if more elusive respondents were excluded, but in contrast to Cordray and Polk found that multivariate relationships were also affected.

Attrition rates will inevitably be high if the researcher fails to maintain contact with the research subjects. Burgess (1989), Clarridge et al. (1977), and Dempster-McClain and Moen (1998) discuss techniques of tracing respondents in some detail. These techniques include obtaining, on the first and subsequent interviews, names and addresses of parents, other relatives, friends, or other individuals with whom the respondent is likely to stay in touch and repeated annual mailings (e.g., birthday cards or other special occasion greeting cards) with a request to the post office to supply a forwarding address if the respondent has moved. City directories, credit agencies, neighborhood visits, and increasingly, as discussed in Dempster-McClain and Moen (1998), resources available on the Internet are also resources that can be employed. To maintain low attrition rates, regardless of the resources available, substantial effort and persistence must be devoted to tracking respondents.

Clarridge et al. (1977), in a 17-year follow-up survey of more than 10,000 Wisconsin high school seniors, were able to locate 97.4% of the original respondents and to obtain interviews from 88.6% of the original sample. Clarridge et al. used a variety of sources, beginning with parents and including colleges and high schools, the post office, military service, neighbors, and friends of the respondents to obtain their high response rates. Burgess (1989) concluded that it was reasonable in surveying most groups in the population to expect to contact or trace 80-90% of all respondents, even over extended time intervals between surveys. One may properly question whether the results of analyses of panel data with attrition rates of 50% or more can reasonably be generalized beyond the respondents who were retained in the study.

To some extent, the impact of panel attrition on the distribution of variables and the substantive findings for a data set may be ascertainable. The binomial test (Bulmer, 1979) may be used to test whether the proportion of individuals in different demographic categories (male or female, white or nonwhite, etc.) changes significantly over time. Other tests of statistical significance may be used to test whether, at the first wave of data collection, those who continued in later waves (stayers) differed from those who were later lost to the study (leavers) with respect to (a) values on particular variables, (b) strength of relationships (e.g., correlations) among variables, or (c) the structure of relationships (e.g., multiple regression equations or covariance structure) among sets of three or more variables. Such tests may uncover evidence of sample variability over successive waves of data collection. Still, it remains possible that some source of sample variability that significantly affects the substantive outcome of the analysis may be overlooked. For example, those with different behavioral trajectories (e.g., increasing as opposed to decreasing drug use) may be differentially likely to remain in or drop out of the panel, and this may not be readily detectable using the methods suggested above. This could seriously bias substantive results such as the estimation and explanation of developmental trends in behavior and be extremely difficult to detect.

In retrospective panel designs, the problem of attrition takes a different form, one not amenable to assessment by the use of tests of statistical significance. Instead of problems associated with respondents leaving the panel after the first wave of data collection, retrospective studies may have problems of selection. Especially for long-term studies, retrospective studies may miss individuals who, for example, died or moved out of the area from which the sample was drawn and who did so during the period for which the data were collected. Those individuals may differ systematically from the rest of the population. For example, frequent users of illicit drugs may have higher mortality than the rest of the population. If this is so, then frequent illicit drug users will be undersampled for the period of the study, and this may bias estimates of change in rates of illicit drug use. In effect, this is a problem of attrition, but it is attrition that takes place before the sample is drawn. It is much more difficult to detect and measure this type of attrition than the attrition that arises in conjunction with prospective panel designs.

Treatment of Missing Data in Longitudinal Research[6]

In longitudinal data, it is possible to have data missing for a single item on a multiple-item scale, for an entire scale, for a particular case at a particular wave but not for all waves (wave nonresponse), or for a particular case for all waves, for example, as a result of initial nonresponse. Regardless of the type of missing data, there is always a risk that it will lead to biased estimation of predictive or causal models or inaccurate estimation of descriptive statistics such as means, standard deviations, or trends. For missing items, if most items in a scale are available, it may be relatively simple to substitute a scale mean for the missing item with some confidence that the resulting estimate is likely to be better than just deleting the case with the missing data from the analysis. When a whole scale is missing, there are several choices, none of them entirely satisfactory, but some at least offering the prospect of improvement over dropping the case entirely. For wave nonresponse or initial nonresponse, if there is a clear pattern of "missingness" by a variable that has been measured (e.g., ethnicity or socioeconomic status), weighting cases so the cases that are most like the missing cases "count" a little more is a frequently used option to reduce potential bias, but it depends on the degree to which the cases that are missing are similar to the nonmissing cases with the same characteristics (again, e.g., ethnicity or socioeconomic status) with respect to other variables and relationships.

Alternatively, one may attempt to adjust the coefficients in a regression or similar model by modeling the nonresponse, particularly if there is reason to believe that the nonrespondents are different from even respondents to whom they appear, based on other variables, to be similar. There are drawbacks to both weighting and modeling nonresponse (Allison, 2002; Brehm, 1993), and in general, it appears that weighting may be preferable when nonresponse rates are low, while modeling nonresponse may be preferable when nonresponse rates are high (e.g., over 30%), but in this latter case, neither is likely to be entirely satisfactory. For wave nonresponse, it may also be possible to fill in some data by interpolation (using both prior and subsequent waves of data to estimate the data at the missing wave) or extrapolation (using only prior waves or only subsequent waves to estimate the missing data). Interpolation or, to a lesser degree, extrapolation, may be reasonable for variables that change little or change in a fairly well-known pattern over time, but it may not be reasonable to use interpolation or especially extrapolation for variables such as attitudes, which may be more volatile over time.

Briefly, there is no one method that is "best" for every type of missing data. All the methods for dealing with missing data make untestable assumptions about the pattern of the missing data or the similarity of missing and nonmissing cases. In some instances, relatively simple methods (e.g., replacing a single missing item with a scale mean when the other items on the scale are nonmissing or weighting cases to compensate for attrition that is linked to an observed, measured characteristic such as ethnicity or socioeconomic status) can be fairly effective. In other instances, one must choose between ease of use and better avoidance of bias, for example, by choosing between the relatively simple (and widely used) technique of listwise deletion or more complex techniques like multiple imputation or regression imputation when data are missing on whole scales or cases in one wave of data. In practical terms, the researcher may be faced with three choices: (1) be a proficient statistician and use maximum likelihood or multiple imputation methods plus selection models for nonresponse, (2) hire a proficient statistician and use maximum likelihood or multiple imputation methods plus selection models for nonresponse, or (3) use listwise deletion. Actually, options (1) and (2) may also result in the use of listwise deletion and weighting cases. For case-missing data, weighting cases often produces results as good as more complex models (Taris, 2000:35-36). For item-missing data, methods such as multiple imputation that are better on average than, for example, listwise deletion, are not always better for specific data sets, as illustrated by examples in Allison (2002), Rovine and Delaney (1990), and Little and Su (1989). Graham and Hofer (2000) suggest that listwise deletion should generally be regarded as acceptable if the resulting loss of cases is small, less than 5%. Allison (2002) also defends the use of listwise deletion as being more robust to violations of the assumption that data are missing at random (MAR) than other methods, including maximum likelihood and multiple imputation (both of which depend on the MAR assumption), in particular for ordinary least squares regression analysis and logistic regression. In general, however, maximum likelihood imputation of missing data on scales or on unscaled items is regarded as preferable to simpler methods such as listwise deletion, at least when the data appear to be truly MAR and also when the proportion of data that are missing is large.

Repeated Measurement and Panel Conditioning

The effect of panel conditioning (e.g., Kalton et al., 1989) in the continued study of a set of respondents is a problem primarily for microsocial, longitudinal panel designs, including experimental and quasi-experimental designs that involve a pretest. Effects of repeated testing may damage internal validity in experimental and quasi-experimental designs, but the use of control groups may allow the researcher to measure this effect and, if it is present, to determine whether there are treatment effects in addition to the changes resulting from repeated measurement. In one example drawn from survey research, the validity of the NCS appears to suffer from effects of repeated interviewing (Cantor, 1989). Mensch and Kandel (1988) found evidence of similar problems in a study of drug use.

Willingness of respondents to answer questions in a way that will evoke a known response (e.g., follow-up questions) is only one threat to validity that emerges with the use of continued study of the same cases. More general unwillingness to participate in the study may also result from continued study and may result in attrition. Yet another possibility is that respondents will change as a result of participation in the survey. Since the introduction of a depression scale in the 1984 wave of the NYS, respondents who reported feeling depressed and having symptoms of depression according to a clinically based depression scale have had the option of requesting an anonymous referral to a mental health professional or facility. The simple fact of having this option may alter the attitudes or behavior of those respondents (who constitute a small proportion of the total sample). Collins et al. (1989) reported that in a study of family caregivers of elderly relatives, 52% identified at least one effect of study participation, most often involving how they (the caregivers) coped with the strains of providing in-home care for their elderly relatives. Rubin and Mitchell (1978) reported that couples in a longitudinal study of the development of relationships were also affected by the research. A common pattern seems to be for the respondents to be more aware of and introspective about their attitudes, emotions, and behavior. It is difficult to tell whether this, in turn, produces substantial changes in attitudes, emotions, or behavior. It is also unclear whether these effects would occur as the result of a single cross-sectional study or whether they are peculiar to longitudinal research involving repeated contact between researchers and respondents.

It is not survey research alone that is susceptible to effects of continued study. Any prospective microsocial research, including observational research, in which there is contact between the researcher and the research subject or in which the subjects are aware that they are being observed risks this type of error. For macrosocial research, depending on how data are collected or accumulated, this may be less of a problem. The length of time for which the United States has been compiling official crime, census, and vital statistics data does not appear to have negatively affected the validity of those data over time. If anything, the opposite is the case. Census coverage has become increasingly complete over the duration of the U.S. census (Robey, 1989). The 1990 census, widely criticized for undercoverage, missed approximately 1.6% of the total population, but it missed more in some demographic groups (as much as 7% of African Americans under 18 years old); preliminary reports indicate that the undercount in the 2000 census is a little over 1%, again with more serious undercoverage for African Americans (Armas, 2001; Hogan & Robinson, 2000). Thoroughness of coverage of police jurisdictions for the FBI Uniform Crime Reports has also increased over time. Similarly, international statistics on population, economic development, and other national characteristics do not appear to have gotten worse over time. Note, too, that retrospective studies may not be susceptible to the problem of continued study (although retrospective studies, like prospective and cross-sectional studies, may have problems if the interview process seems too long and tedious to the respondents).

The problem of continued study of a panel of subjects is thus primarily of concern for microsocial, prospective studies. Even for microsocial, prospective studies, it may be possible to avoid the problem, either by adjusting the interval between data collection waves (the 1- to 3-year interval used in the NYS, as opposed to the 6-month interval used in the NCS), by varying the design of the questionnaire from wave to wave (although that may raise another set of issues regarding the comparability of data from one wave of data collection to another) or by successfully encouraging a high level of commitment to the research on the part of subjects and research staff.

Respondent Recall

A good general review of the research on short- versus long-term retrospective recall data is provided by Rutter et al. (1998). Research on short- versus long-term retrospective data typically indicates that (a) memories tend to fade with time; (b) short- and long-term recall data on more salient events or attitudes tend to be more consistent than data on less salient events or attitudes; (c) short- and long-term recall data on objective events or characteristics tend to be more consistent than data on attitudes or other psychological data; and (d) differences between short- and long-term recall data indicate that the long-term recall data tend to be biased to reflect respondents' current views and attitudes. Regarding this last point, people tend to reconstruct and reinterpret their memories to reflect their current life situations and attitudes, in effect constructing a consistent "life story" for themselves. This is not to say that long-term recall data are consistently unreliable or invalid, but it does suggest that they should be used with caution and that, whenever possible, the shorter term recall data characteristic of prospective longitudinal designs is to be preferred.

The potential consequence of this is to generate inconsistencies when prospective (or, more accurately, short-term recall) and retrospective (or long-term recall) data are compared for the same subjects. For example, Henry et al. (1994) compared retrospective respondent report data to prospective data based on both archival records and respondent reports for a wide range of conceptual domains, including physical characteristics (height, weight), residential mobility, family relationships, contacts with police, reading ability, and psychological well-being. They found that retrospective measures of psychological or attitudinal variables (e.g., family relationships) were least consistent with prospective data, while measurement of objective characteristics (e.g., residence changes or police contacts) were relatively consistent with prospective data. Even when correlations between the retrospective and prospective data were high, absolute differences were sometimes large.

Sorenson et al. (1989) argued that retrospective designs provided accurate accounts of past delinquent behavior. To draw this inference, however, they relied on a comparison of cross-sectional surveys from two different populations (Contra Costa County, California, in 1965 and the St. Louis, Missouri, metropolitan area in 1981 and 1982). Based on the fact that the cross-sectional data for St. Louis in 1965 (collected retrospectively in 1981-1982) produced similar rates of illegal behavior to those found in the Contra Costa County data (collected prospectively) for 1965, they concluded that the retrospective data for St. Louis were valid. The defect of such an argument is that any similarity between the two may be a fortuitous combination of trends in the two areas that produce coincident rates in a particular period. In particular, if Contra Costa County had lower rates of illegal behavior in 1965 than St. Louis, and if the retrospective data for St. Louis underreported past illegal behavior, the two might agree on rates of illegal behavior despite problems in the validity of the retrospective data. A much better procedure would be to compare prospective and retrospective data from the same respondents.

Menard and Elliott (1990a) used data from the NYS to compare (a) trends in the prevalence of offending (the percentage of the respondents in the sample who reported having committed a particular offense) based on 1-, 2-, and 3-year recall periods, and (b) the prevalence of serious offending based on prospective data with a 1-year recall period and retrospective data with a variable recall period (typically 10 years). Comparisons of 1-, 2-, and 3-year recall periods for general nondrug offending, serious (Index) nondrug offending, marijuana use, and other illicit drug use (polydrug use) are illustrated in Figure 4.1. The solid lines represent trends based on the prospective, 1-year recall data for 1976-83 (annual data were not available for 1981 and 1982; the solid lines simply connect the data points for 1980 and 1983). The dashed lines represent trends based on 3-year recall data for 1981 and 2-year recall for 1982 (and connected to the data points for 1980

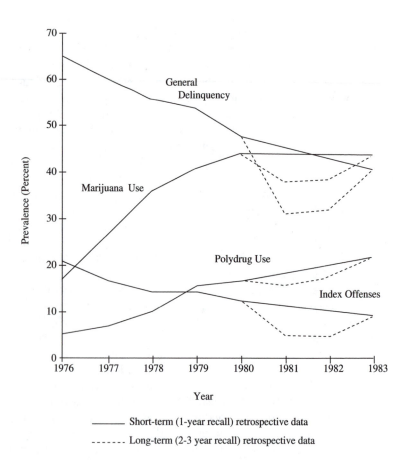

Figure 4.1. Period Trends Based on Long- and Short-Term Recall

and 1983). For 1981-83, the prospective data (based on 1980 and 1983) indicate stable or declining trends for general offending, Index offending, and marijuana use, but the extended recall data (for 1981 and 1982) indicate positive trends. For polydrug use, the extended recall data do not deviate a great deal from the 1-year recall data, but for all four types of illegal behavior, there is a "dipper" effect, with trend lines based on long-term recall data dipping below the trend lines for the 1-year recall data. Figure 4.1 is consistent with a pattern of increased forgetting as the interval over which the respondent is asked to remember events or behavior increases. The problem of memory decay appears less serious for some types of illegal behavior (hard drug use) than for others (general nondrug offending).

Menard and Elliott considered other possible explanations of this pattern but concluded that increased memory decay with increasing length of the interval over which respondents are asked to remember events was the most plausible explanation.

In the comparison of prospective (1-year recall) and retrospective (10-year recall) data, the same respondents were asked whether (and if so, when) they had ever committed each of several serious offenses (rape, robbery, aggravated assault, gang fighting, burglary, theft of over $50, motor vehicle theft, and sale of hard drugs). Briefly, the prospective self-reports included over 90% of the offenses reported on the retrospective self-reports, but the retrospective self-reports captured fewer than half the offenses found by the prospective self-reports. These results are also consistent with the hypothesis of increasing memory decay for longer intervals. Other possible explanations for these patterns were examined by Menard and Elliott (1990a) but were again found to be less plausible than the explanation based on failure to remember events that occurred several years ago. Although these results do not rule out the use of retrospective data in general, it is clear that for some behaviors, long-term retrospective data are unreliable and may produce trends or effects opposite to those indicated by prospective data.

Issues of replication and recall may also include the phenomena of telescoping and reverse telescoping: reporting an event that happened in one period for a more or less recent period than the one in which it occurred. Evidence of telescoping has been found in the NCS (Lehnen & Skogan, 1981), and the first interview for NCS respondents is not used for estimating rates of victimization for the sample. Other studies attempt to use memory-bounding techniques (e.g., reference to particular events such as birthdays or holidays) to reduce the impact of telescoping and reverse telescoping. The data from the NYS (Menard & Elliott, 1990a) also indicate some telescoping and reverse telescoping when retrospective and prospective data are compared.

Attempts have been made to reduce errors associated with respondent recall of whether or when events occurred. These include the use of introductory material to prepare the respondent for the question; asking more detailed questions (rather than asking one question about whether the respondent has ever broken the law, asking a series of questions about specific offenses); providing clear reference periods bounded by easily remembered dates (e.g., holidays, presidential elections, or major news events); and attempting to link the events about which the question is being asked with salient events in the respondent's life, for example, by showing the respondent a calendar for the period about which questions are being asked and asking the respondent to fill in important life events during that period

(Converse & Presser, 1986; Fowler, 1998). An expansion of this latter approach is the use of "life history calendars" (Freedman et al., 1988), in which respondents were presented with a calendar (with dates across the top and one line for each event or characteristic about which the respondent is being asked) and asked to locate the events in which the researcher is interested on that calendar. This approach, as noted by Freedman et al. (1988), involves potentially costly and tedious coding, and it appears much better suited for retrospective recall of events (e.g., birth of a child or change of residence) or conditions (enrollment in school or marital status) than for attitudinal data. Reviewing research on the life history calendar (LHC), Taris (2000:11, italics in original) concludes, "It seems fair to say that the LHC improves recall *sometimes* for *some* variables, but certainly not *always* for *all* variables. A prospective longitudinal design will virtually always result in better (more reliable and more accurate) data than a retrospective design."

Problems of respondent recall are problems primarily for microsocial interview research. The use of prospective panel designs helps to reduce these problems but not to eliminate them altogether. Retrospective designs may have serious problems of validity because as the length of the time interval for which respondents are asked to report events or behavior increases, so does the likelihood of memory failure, memory reconstruction (Weis, 1986), and underreporting. For some purposes, such as measuring changes in attitudes over time, only prospective panel designs appear to be adequate. Finally, caution should be exercised when using repeated cross-sectional designs to measure change over time. Even relatively minor differences in sampling procedures or the administration of survey instruments may produce serious problems for replication, as Martin's (1983) examples indicate.

The Costs of Longitudinal Research

Wall and Williams (1970) suggested that the costs of prospective panel studies are probably no higher per wave of data collected than the costs of a similar number of cross-sectional studies. Six waves of a prospective longitudinal survey may cost no more than six cross-sectional studies with comparable populations and sample sizes. Although this may be true, it is important to consider whether one six-wave prospective longitudinal study is worth as much as or more than six separate cross-sectional studies or worth six times as much as a retrospective panel study. Not all types of research require longitudinal data, and some that do could rely on secondary analysis of longitudinal data that have already been collected by other researchers.

For some purposes, longitudinal research is the only acceptable option. If the purpose is to measure historical or developmental change, a longitudinal design is essential, especially to separate age, period, and cohort effects. If change is to be measured over a long span of time, then a prospective panel design or total population design will usually be the most appropriate design for the research, because independent samples (in repeated cross-sectional designs) may differ from one another unless both formal and informal procedures for sampling and data collection are faithfully replicated for each wave of data (Martin, 1983). Also, recall failure may render inferences drawn from retrospective panel designs invalid. If change is to be measured over a relatively short time (weeks or months), then a retrospective design may be appropriate for data on events or behaviors but probably not for attitudes or beliefs. Repeated cross-sectional designs or revolving panel designs may be appropriate if a problem of panel conditioning as a result of repeated interviewing or observation in a prospective panel is anticipated.

If the purpose of the research is to identify or estimate the strength of causal relationships, longitudinal research may again be preferable to cross-sectional research, especially if the true causal and temporal order of changes in variables is unknown. Hypotheses derived from theory or, worse, guesses about correct causal and temporal order, are inadequate substitutes for knowledge about causal and temporal order, and temporal order is one aspect of a relationship that must be tested to determine whether a proposed causal relationship exists. The best tests of causal relationships involve the use of experimental designs (Bickman & Rog, 1998; Campbell & Stanley, 1963; Rossi et al., 1999), and experimental designs are at least implicitly, and usually explicitly, prospective longitudinal designs.

If the measurement of change is not a concern, if causal and temporal order are known, or if there is no concern with causal relationships, then cross-sectional data and analysis may be sufficient. If, however, the research problem requires longitudinal data and analysis, it makes more sense to spend more money to get the right answer than to spend less money to get an answer that may well be wrong or at best inconclusive. Under such circumstances, the question of whether longitudinal research is worth the cost does not really involve a question of whether longitudinal or cross-sectional methods should be used; it involves a question of whether the cost of the longitudinal research is justified by the importance of the research problem being considered. The choice should be between doing the research properly or not doing it at all.

5. LONGITUDINAL ANALYSIS

In Chapter 2, two primary purposes for longitudinal research were described: the description of patterns of change and the analysis of causal relationships. This final chapter presents a broad overview of analytical methods for accomplishing these purposes. In so doing, the chapter shifts from a focus on longitudinal *data collection* to a focus on longitudinal *data analysis*, what to do with the data once they are collected. The various methods for longitudinal data analysis are fully described elsewhere, and it is not the purpose of this chapter to demonstrate in detail how to use each method. Instead, the focus is on the different types of research questions that may be addressed by longitudinal research and the different methods that may be used to answer those questions. More detailed explication of the methods of longitudinal analysis may be found in the sources cited in connection with the respective methods. For a general introduction to longitudinal analysis, see Taris (2000) and Bijleveld et al. (1998).

For the first purpose, describing change, it is important to make distinctions between (1) qualitative and quantitative change, (2) short-term (few periods, regardless of the actual length of a single period) and long-term (many periods) change, (3) whether the change in which we are interested is a change in values of one or more variables or a change in the relationship between two or more variables, and (4) whether we are interested in describing, predicting, or explaining change. With respect to the fourth point, describing change typically involves a bivariate relationship between time or age and some variable of interest. Predicting change may involve no more than a simple forecast based only on time trends, or it may involve more complex models with multiple predictors of change. Explaining change requires the addition of assumptions and theory about the causal interrelationships among the variables and moves us into the realm of the second purpose for longitudinal research, causal analysis.

In causal analysis, we also need to make distinctions between (1) qualitative and quantitative outcomes, (2) short-term and long-term analysis, and (3) whether we are interested in the value of a particular outcome or in the relationship of two or more outcomes to each other. Notice the use of the word *outcome* in place of the word *change* here. The fourth distinction for causal analysis is (4) whether we are interested in the *change* in a variable over some *span* of time or in *differences* between cases in the value or level of the outcome at some *point* in time. Either the change within the case (e.g., *intraindividual change*, when the cases are people) or the differences between cases (e.g., *interindividual differences*) may be of interest in causal analysis. For example, are we more interested in the causes of differences between countries in their total fertility rates, as they may be affected by per capita gross national product, literacy, and public funding for family planning efforts, or in the *change* in the total fertility rate in one or more nations after the introduction of a new family planning program? Similarly, are we more interested in differences between adolescents' frequency of marijuana use (e.g., the number of times they use marijuana in a year) or in changes in individual frequency of marijuana use as they get older or are exposed to an antidrug intervention? These are distinctly different questions, and they have different implications for how we should measure and analyze the outcome in which we are interested.

Three somewhat oversimplified illustrations may be useful here, involving *experimental and quasi-experimental* research, *developmental* research, and *causal analysis of differences*. In most *experimental and quasi-experimental* research, the concern is with short-term change. Baseline measurements are taken, an intervention is performed with some subjects (the treatment group) but not with others (the comparison group), and a second set of measurements is taken after the intervention has had time to produce an effect. The question of interest is whether the treatment group experienced a *change* that was different in direction or magnitude from any change experienced by the comparison group. Experimental and quasi-experimental research in the social sciences often has an applied or practical focus. For example, did the students exposed to the new curriculum learn more than students exposed to a standard curriculum, or were unemployed teenagers who were given training in job-seeking skills more likely to find employment than teenagers without such training? The focus is often, but not always, on short-term analysis of change.

Although *developmental* research sometimes considers short-term patterns of change, it is more often concerned with longer term change, particularly change over the life course or a substantial part of the life course. Examples include the development of quantitative skills from preschool through the end of high school or involvement in illegal behavior from preadolescence to middle adulthood or old age. Instead of being interested in the change between two specific periods, we are interested in the *pattern* of change over (preferably) a relatively large number of periods: whether it increases and never diminishes, even though it may perhaps level off at some point (as we might expect for the development of quantitative skills) or whether it first increases, then declines (as is typical of involvement in illegal behavior). In addition to describing this pattern, we may want to see whether either the pattern itself (the relationship between the outcome and time) or the eventual level of quantitative skills or involvement in illegal behavior (the level or value of the outcome, measured, e.g., at age 21) differs systematically for individuals who have different characteristics (e.g., gender, ethnicity, socioeconomic status).

Developmental research is particularly useful for studying individuals, for whom there may be relatively clear beginnings (birth, first year of school, first job) and endings (death, completion of formal education, retirement). It may also be useful for studying macrosocial entities such as cities or nations, which do not always have clear (or at least not clearly observed) beginnings and endings for many variables of interest (fertility and mortality rates, literacy, and per capita gross national product, to parallel the examples used at the individual level). At both the individual and macrosocial levels, however, we may sometimes be less interested in the pattern of change over age or time than in the level or value of an outcome at some specific age or time. A classic example is Blau and Duncan's (1966) study of men's occupational status attainment at a specific time (1962, for ages 20-64), as a function of their father's education and occupation, their own education, and the occupational status of their own first jobs. While there is a concern with change here (change in occupational status from father's job to son's job or from son's first job to son's current job), much of the focus in this and subsequent research on status attainment (Grusky, 2001, Part IV) has been on explaining why *levels* of occupational status are higher for some individuals than for others. Let us call this the *causal analysis of differences* (implicitly, differences between individuals, not differences within individuals over time) to distinguish it from the (causal or other) analysis of change.

It is important that although applied/experimental and developmental research requires repeated measurements on the same cases (whether individuals or total populations), repeated measurement is an option but not a requirement for causal analysis of differences. In principle, time-ordered cross-sectional models could be (and have been) used, for example, in the status attainment research described in the preceding paragraph, and as noted earlier it has been used in cross-national research on fertility, family planning, and development (Tolnay & Christenson, 1984). Longitudinal data, whether based on total population, repeated cross-sectional, or extended recall panel designs, are still useful in the causal analysis of differences and offer advantages over purely cross-sectional (or even time-ordered cross-sectional) data.

Longitudinal Versus Cross-Sectional Statistical Models

Assume that we have selected a theoretically appropriate set of dependent and independent variables. Assume further that we have agreed upon the causal ordering of the variables, based on theory and perhaps with empirical support based on past research. Assume further that we have been able, with appropriate transformations of our variables, to cast the causal model into a general linear model (e.g., latent variable structural equations, multiple regression, analysis of variance [ANOVA] and analysis of covariance [ANCOVA], logistic regression, or discriminant analysis), and that the model is identified (see Heise, 1975, for a discussion of model identification). Suppose now that we want to calculate the strength of the direct causal relationships (and if we use path analysis or latent variable structural equation models, we may also calculate indirect effects). Is there any reason to prefer longitudinal data instead of cross-sectional data for this purpose?

Schoenberg (1977) demonstrated that under certain conditions, the application of dynamic models to cross-sectional data produced efficient, unbiased estimates of the parameters of the underlying dynamic model. The fundamental condition for this to occur was that the underlying dynamic process be *nonergodic*, that is, that it depend on the initial state of the system. For *ergodic* systems, systems that do not depend on the initial state of the system but that would result in an identical expected state of the system for any time period, the calculation of a dynamic model based on cross-sectional data results in biased and inefficient estimates of parameters.

An example of an ergodic system is one in which changes in the exogenous variables are random and the expected values of the exogenous variables are the same at any time t as at any other time $(t - k)$. Mathematically, $E(X_t) = X_0$, where X_0 is the initial value of X. An example of a nonergodic system is one in which changes in the independent variables are not random but depend on past values of the exogenous variable. In other words, an autoregressive process, in addition to random variation, generates the values of the exogenous variables, and the expected value of X is not constant. Mathematically, $E(X_t) = \Sigma \phi_k X_{t-k}$, where for $k = 1, 2, \ldots, K$, the X_{t-k} are past values of X and the ϕ_k are coefficients for the respective X_{t-k}. Whether cross-sectional data may be used to calculate the dynamic relationship between the exogenous variables (X) and the dependent variable (Y) would depend on which process, random variation or autoregression, produced the changes in X. By contrast, longitudinal models may be used for both ergodic and nonergodic processes.

A second potential problem with using cross-sectional data to estimate parameters for a longitudinal model is illustrated by Firebaugh (1980) with data on fertility and literacy. Table 5.1 and Figure 5.1, both adapted from Firebaugh (1980:340-341), illustrate that cross-sectional and longitudinal correlations may be opposite in sign, and yet may both be correct. Cross-sectionally, fertility was highest in those districts of the Punjab in India with the highest levels of literacy, beginning in 1961 and continuing through 1971. Within each district, however, as literacy increased over time, fertility declined. In this example, cross-sectional and longitudinal data produce very

TABLE 5.1

Cross-Sectional and Longitudinal Correlations Between
Fertility and Literacy: The Punjab, India, 1961 to 1971

Time series correlations (within districts over time)		Cross-sectional correlations (within years across districts)	
District	*Correlation*	*Year*	*Correlation*
Amritsar	−.9	1961	.5
Bhatinda	−.5	1962	.6
Ferozepur	−.9	1963	.4
Gurdaspur	−.9	1964	.6
Hoshiarpur	−.8	1965	.1
Jullundur	−.7	1966	.2
Kapurthala	−.4	1967	.3
Ludhiana	−.9	1968	.6
Patiala	−.3	1969	.5
Ropar	−.4	1970	.6
Sangrur	−.1	1971	.7

different conclusions about the relationship between fertility and literacy. As noted earlier, a similar pattern was found by Menard and Elliott (1990a) and Greenberg (1985) with regard to the relationship between age and illegal behavior. As Firebaugh remarks, determining which of the two patterns is more appropriate or important is a theoretical issue, not an empirical issue, but the point here is that cross-sectional data cannot be routinely used to model dynamic, longitudinal relationships. This point is further reinforced by Menard and Elliott (1990a) based on actual cross-sectional and longitudinal data and by Davies and Pickles (1985), who demonstrated in a simulation study of a dynamic model that cross-sectional analysis failed to make correct inferences about predefined population parameters, but longitudinal analysis estimates were well within the limits of sampling error.

Types of Longitudinal Causal Models

There are four "pure" types of causal models: (A) $X \rightarrow Y$, the value of the dependent variable is expressed as a function of the value of the independent variable; (B) $\Delta X \rightarrow Y$, where ΔX represents a change in X, and the value of the dependent variable is expressed as a function of the change in the independent variable; (C) $X \rightarrow \Delta Y$, where ΔY represents a change in Y and the change in the dependent variable is expressed as a function of the value of the independent variable; and (D) $\Delta X \rightarrow \Delta Y$ the change in the dependent variable is expressed as a function of the change in the independent variable. Mixed

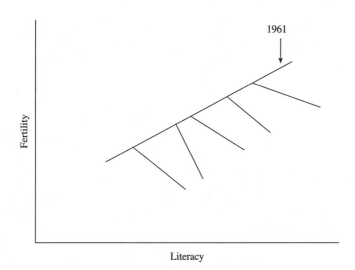

1961

Fertility

Literacy

Figure 5.1. General Pattern of the Relationship Between Fertility and Literacy

models, in which (for example) the independent variables include both level and rate-of-change variables (e.g., population density and population growth rate as influences on economic development) are also possible.

In causal analysis with cross-sectional data, we often phrase our hypotheses as though we were testing model D: a change in X produces (leads to, causes) a change in Y. More typically, however, it is model A that we test in cross-sectional *and* longitudinal analysis. Correctly phrased, model A indicates that the *level* or value of one variable (the dependent variable) depends on the level or value of one or more independent variables. Phrased another way, *differences* in X produce *differences* in Y, for example, differences in salary result in differences in job satisfaction or differences in literacy rates produce differences in fertility rates. This *implies* that a change in the dependent variable is also a function of change in the independent variable, for example, that a change in salary produces a change in job satisfaction, but the actual formulation of the model to be tested involves values of variables, not changes in these values.

In addition, it is possible that a change in one variable produces a systematic change in another but that the values of the two variables are largely unrelated. This suggests a process in which the initial values of X and Y were independent, but changes in X produce changes in Y. For example, levels of nutrition (as measured by per capita calorie supply) may initially be unrelated to levels of national family planning program effort (countries with both high and low levels of nutrition have both high and low levels of family planning program effort), but increases in family planning program effort may lead to increases in per capita calorie supply, as individuals more effectively adjust their fertility, deliberately or inadvertently, to the carrying capacity of their country or region. High levels of family planning program effort are still not necessarily associated with high levels of nutrition, but improvements in family planning program effort are associated with improvements in nutrition. The process described here is admittedly counterintuitive, but nonetheless possible. If such a process exists, then model D is appropriate, but model A is not. Model D, on the other hand, may be appropriate in any situation for which A is appropriate. If the level of one variable influences the level of another, then if the first variable changes, the second must also (i.e., the change in the second variable depends on the change in the first, if model A is correct). Analytically, model D may result from the use of first difference or unconditional change models (Finkel, 1995; Liker et al., 1985).

An example of the pure form of model B might be the correspondence between the level of stress (as a dependent variable) and the amount of change in income (a big pay raise produces low stress, a big pay cut produces high stress, regardless of initial level of income). Model C suggests that a rate of change depends on some difference, possibly a stable difference. For example, the rate of increase in salary may depend on stable characteristics such as ethnicity in an ethnically biased organization or educational attainment, measured by highest grade or degree completed, in a meritocratic organization. Model C is one possible form for a differential equation model. For example, Richardson (1960) explained arms races between pairs of countries by using pairs of differential equations:

$$dX/dt = kY - aX + g \quad \text{and} \quad dY/dt = jX - bY + h$$

where X and Y represent levels of armaments in the two countries, j and k represent nonnegative "defense" coefficients (positive influences on the felt need for arms, based on the level of armaments in the other country), a and b represented nonnegative "fatigue" coefficients (the drain on the national economy or unwillingness to build up one's own armaments further, given the level of armaments already present in one's own country), and g and h are constant, positive or negative "grievance" factors that may loosely be interpreted as the hostility (if they are positive) or friendliness (if they are negative) each country feels toward the other. The right-hand sides of the equations, dX/dt and dY/dt, represent rates of change over time; the left-hand sides of the equations are expressed in terms of levels of X and Y.

Model C was also used by Mauldin and Berelson (1978) in a regression analysis to explain changes in crude birth rates in less developed countries.

With change in crude birth rate as the dependent variable, levels of family planning program effort and indicators of social and economic development were used as the independent variables. Tsui and Bogue (1978) performed a similar analysis with similar variables but used model A with a lagged endogenous variable. As Markus (1979) explains, the use of a change score, $(Y_2 - Y_1)$, as the dependent variable is the same as using a lagged endogenous variable except that in the model with the change score as the dependent variable, the coefficient of the lagged endogenous variable is assumed to be 1. For the lagged endogenous model with dependent variable Y and independent variable X (and where the subscripts refer to time of measurement), $Y_2 = a + bX + cY_1$; or, recalculating, $(Y_2 - cY_1) = a + bX$. If $c = 1$, then the equation takes the form of a standard regression model, with the change score $(Y_2 - Y_1)$ as the dependent variable. Given the similarity in the change score and lagged endogenous variable approaches, it is not surprising that Mauldin and Berelson (1978) and Tsui and Bogue (1978) reached practically identical substantive conclusions; even the explained variance in the dependent variables was practically identical. Markus (1979) suggests that there is nothing to be gained by constraining the coefficient c in the above model to be equal to 1 and recommends using the lagged endogenous variable instead of the change score as a dependent variable.

In all of these models, but particularly for models A and D, the timing of measurement is an issue. When $X \rightarrow \Delta Y$ (model C), presumably X should be measured for a period before the beginning of the change in Y, and when $\Delta X \rightarrow Y$ (model B), the time span during which the change in X is measured should end before the period for which Y is measured. For $\Delta X \rightarrow \Delta Y$, however, a case could be made for measuring the changes in X and Y contemporaneously (instantaneous effect), for measuring the change in X for a time span that ends before the change in Y begins (lagged effect), or, in between the previous two possibilities, measuring the change in X for a time span that begins before Y begins to change but ends after Y has begun to change (partially lagged effect). Similarly for $X \rightarrow Y$ (model A), one needs to consider whether X should be measured for a period prior to the period for which Y is measured (lagged effect) or for the same period for which Y is measured (instantaneous effect).

Measuring Change

Measuring or describing change, at its most basic level, involves a bivariate relationship between two variables, one measuring chronological time or age and another measuring some outcome of interest. This apparently simple task can sometimes be deceptively difficult, in terms of selecting the most appropriate measure of change. First, a distinction needs to be made between qualitative and quantitative change. The measurement of qualitative change is straightforward: Either there is a change in the value of the variable (i.e., in qualitative states), or there is not. For example, one either moves from being a nondelinquent (no delinquent activity) to being a delinquent (some delinquent activity), or one remains a nondelinquent. One moves from being a blue-collar worker to being a white-collar worker, or one remains a blue-collar worker. For each separate category of each variable, the pattern is the same: One either changes or one does not. Measurement of purely qualitative change may thus involve a simple yes-no dichotomy. If categories are ordinal and few in number, the dichotomous measurement of change is adequate, but for ordinal scales with many categories a more detailed, quantitative measure of change may be feasible or desirable. More extensive specification of *how* a case has changed may be desirable (e.g., for the nominal scale "religion," we may want to know whether one converted from Protestantism to Roman Catholicism or to Judaism), but in principle this just means constructing a set of categories based on different dichotomous possibilities of change (one for each state at time 1 and one for each corresponding state at time 2). *Whether* there has been any change is still a dichotomous measure.

For continuous measurement scales, two measures of change are commonly considered. One is the *difference* between the later score and the earlier score on a variable as defined by subtraction: $X_2 - X_1$, where the subscripts refer to time periods. This may be called a difference, a *change score*, a *raw change*, or a *raw gain*. A second measure that has been used in research on change is the *residual gain*. In order to calculate a residual gain, the variable Y_2 is first regressed (using linear regression) on Y_1 in order to obtain a predicted or *expected* value for Y_2. The expected value of Y_2, $E(Y_2)$, depends on the value of Y_1 and the values of two parameters, a (the intercept; the expected value of Y_2 when Y_1 is zero) and b (the slope of the best fitting line for describing the relationship between Y_2 and Y_1): $E(Y_2) = a + bY_1$. The residual gain score is the difference between the actual value of Y_2 and the expected or predicted value of Y_2: Residual gain $(Y) = Y_2 - E(Y_2) = Y_2 - a - bY_1$.

For ratio scales, there is a third commonly used measure of change. The *percent change* in Z is: Percent change $(Z) = 100\%(Z_2 - Z_1)/Z_1$. This measure is not appropriate for use with anything other than a ratio scale because for any scale without a nonarbitrary zero point, there exist an infinite number of different but equally valid measures of percent change. To illustrate this point, consider temperature as an example. On this interval scale, the percent change from room temperature to the boiling point of water is

100%(212 − 70)/70 = 203% for the Fahrenheit scale, but for the Celsius scale it is 100%(100 − 21)/21 = 376%. Also, when $Z_1 = 0$, the percent change cannot be calculated because division by zero is not permitted. Variations on percent change as a measure of change include measures based on rates other than percentages (e.g., rates per 1,000 or per 100,000) and the compound rate of change, the most familiar example of which is the compounding of interest in a savings account. A measure of change may be based on more than one unit of time. One simply divides the change by the number of periods (or other units of time, not necessarily equal in length to the periods used for measurement) over which the change occurs in order to obtain a *rate of change*: a raw gain, residual gain, or percent change, measured per unit time, such as the average annual percent change in the crime rate or in per capita income.

The description of a pattern of change may typically take one of three forms: numerical, graphical, or mathematical (including statistical). Numerical descriptions of change simply involve the presentation of the numerical value of some measure of change, for example, the annual per- cent change in the per capita gross national product. Describing change using simple measures such as these is more characteristic of short-term experimental and quasi-experimental research and less characteristic of developmental research. Graphical descriptions of change generally involve plotting values of a variable for different periods on a graph on which time is the horizontal axis and the variable is represented on the vertical axis. Figure 4.1, presented earlier, is an example of a graphical depiction of change and indicates whether trends are upward, downward, or stable for any given time span and whether and how trends change at different times. Mathematical and statistical models of change describe change in terms of an equation relating change to time. Models of quantitative change focus on *how much* a variable changes over time, while models of qualitative change focus on *how many cases* change in certain ways over time.

Issues in the Measurement of Change. Any of the change measures described above may be used for either individual cases or for groups of cases (e.g., males and females, more developed and less developed countries) in total population designs, panel designs, and (for some cases over a limited span of time) revolving panel designs. In repeated cross-sectional designs, measurement of change for individual cases is not really possible, but change may be measured for well-defined groups of cases as long as the cases are comparable at the group level from one cross-section to the next. For probability samples of the population with adequate numbers of cases in each group, this should pose little problem as long as sampling and the administration of the data collection are strictly replicated, but any devia- tion from the original sampling or administration procedures may seriously compromise the comparability of the data and may render the repeated cross-sectional data useless for longitudinal analysis (Martin, 1983). All the longitudinal designs described in Figure 3.1 may be used to measure change for the full sample or population, but again with repeated cross-sectional designs care must be taken to be sure that the sampling and administration procedures are the same for different cross-sections.

Whenever we attempt to measure change, we need to consider whether apparent differences from one time to another really indicate change or whether they may indicate unreliability of measurement instead. Previously cited examples illustrate this problem. Were the different conclusions of Redfield (1930) and Lewis (1951) in Tepoztlan, Mexico, the result of unreliability (one or both of the observers were biased and gave an inaccurate account of life in the village), or did the village change substantially in the time from Redfield's observation to the time when Lewis conducted his research? Does the negative association between number of times interviewed and number of victimization incidents reported in the National Crime Survey (Cantor, 1989) reflect unreliability in the National Crime Survey data, a real decline (possibly the result of a "treatment" effect in which responding to the survey provokes respondents to think about their victimization experiences more deeply and to take precautions to avoid victimization), a sampling problem (are those with the highest rates of victimization disproportionately likely to change households and thus to leave the sample?), or a real period trend in victimization? The characteristics of the sample with respect to length of time in the sample would presumably have stabilized in 1976 (i.e., the number of respondents or households that had been interviewed once, twice, three times, etc. would be expected to remain the same after the first 3 years because the sample revolves on a 3-year cycle) and estimated victimization rates for most offenses declined in the National Crime Survey panel after 1976 (Bureau of Justice Statistics, 1992; Rennison, 2000). It is thus possible that some of the decline in victimization rates measured on repeated interviews is attributable to real period trends in victimization, but it is unlikely that period trends can explain all the observed change (Cantor, 1989). Interestingly, it is possible that trends in victimization are measured more accurately than levels of victimization because since 1976 the National Crime Survey has probably had the same distribution of systematic error within the sample.

Recall that test-retest reliability measures (but not internal consistency reliability measures) are themselves measures of change when it is assumed that no change has actually occurred (Zeller & Carmines, 1980). The dilemma of separating unreliability of measurement from real change may best be addressed by replication and the use of multiple, independent measures of reliability and change. In some instances, other evidence may clearly favor one explanation (e.g., unreliability) over the other (e.g., change). For example, changes in prevalence of illegal behavior may be similar across age groups in an age-specific analysis, and these changes may be independent of the number of previous interviews; this would suggest real change instead of unreliability. If changes varied across age groups in a way that appeared to be linked with the number of previous interviews, a stronger case could be made for unreliability.

Describing Changes in Relationships Among Variables. Up to this point, the focus has been on changes in the value of one or more variables over time, and this is usually the primary concern in the description of change over time. It is also possible, however, to examine changes in the *relationships* among variables over time. Payne et al. (1994) illustrate this with two examples, one using logistic regression to see how the relationship between job qualifications and unemployment changes over time and a second example using loglinear analysis to examine how the relationship between social class and political party changes over time. In the first example, they found that the disadvantage for individuals having no job qualifications changed over time and more specifically was higher in an earlier period when unemployment was higher than in a later period when unemployment was lower. In the second example, parallel to the study cited earlier by Hout et al. (1999) for the United States, they found that in British elections, the association between social class and political party affiliation declined over time. Both of these examples involve causal or at least predictive models, but note that the focus is on the change in the relationship of the dependent or outcome variable to its predictors, as much as or more than on how well the predictors predict the outcome variable. Also, as is commonly the case in the analysis of changes in relationships over time, some attempt is made to explain that change in terms of historical or developmental changes in other variables.

Similar analysis can be performed using structural equation modeling, for example, using stacked models for different periods to test for equality of structural parameters over time. Especially important in this context is testing for *factorial invariance* (e.g., Kaplan, 2000, chap. 4; Patterson, 1995), whether the same indicators have the same relationship to underlying concepts at one time as at another. The issue of factorial invariance is one type of question that arises in considering whether measurement is constant over time. As noted earlier, even using the same measurements over time does not always mean that we are measuring the same thing in each period. Patterson (1995) gives the example of the antisocial trait as a concept whose manifest indicators change as the individual gets older and illustrates how the different components of deviancy change from fourth to eighth grade, as substance use and official contact with police increase in importance. As illustrated by Patterson, especially in life course research, different variables may measure the same thing at different stages of development.

Deterministic Versus Probabilistic Models

Mathematical and statistical models may be *deterministic* or *probabilistic*. In a deterministic descriptive model of change, all cases having a specified set of characteristics are expected to change in exactly the same way. In deterministic causal models, knowing the values of some relevant, finite set of predictor variables, or whether or how much they change for a specific case, permits us to know with (in principle) certainty the value of a predicted or dependent variable, whether it will change, how it will change (increase or decrease), and by how much it will change for that case. In practice, in the social sciences, there is likely to be some deviation from predictions of deterministic models, if only as a result of measurement error. Deterministic models of change in quantitative variables in the social sciences include functional equations (Kim & Roush, 1980:101-104), difference equations (Huckfeldt et al., 1982; Kim & Roush, 1980, chap. 5), and differential equation models (Blalock, 1969:88-91; Kim & Roush, 1980, chap. 6). All these models express the values of the variable in which change is being described as functions of time. *Descriptions* of change in a variable should include only that variable and time in the mathematical formula; *explanations* of change involve the introduction of other variables into the equation; and *predictions* of change may or may not involve predictors other than time.

The Richardson (1960) arms race model described earlier is an example of a deterministic causal model that attempts to explain changes in levels of armaments. An example of a deterministic descriptive model of change is the *internal-influence diffusion model* (Mahajan & Peterson, 1985). Simple models of the diffusion of an innovation such as the internal-influence diffusion model typically express the cumulative number of adopters of an innovation at a given time as a function of time, expressible in the form of a differential equation (Hamblin et al., 1973; Mahajan & Peterson, 1985). One possible equation for describing this process is $dX/dt = ct^n$, where X is the cumulative number who have adopted an innovation, dX/dt is the rate of change in X, t is time measured in some appropriate unit, and n and c are constant parameters that need to be estimated. If we integrate the equation, it may be written equivalently as $X = ct^{n+1}/(n + 1)$. In its simplest form, if $n = 0$, the equation becomes $X = ct$; X is expressed as a linear function of time, and the constant c may be estimated by using ordinary least squares regression techniques. This approach, or variations with polynomial functions of t, may be useful for describing change when the number of cases is relatively large (e.g., more than 20) and the number of measurement periods is relatively small.

In a probabilistic descriptive model of change, what we expect is not that all cases will change in the same way, even if they have the same characteristics, but that a certain proportion of cases will change in a certain way. In probabilistic causal models, if we know the values of some relevant, finite set of predictor variables or how they change for the total population, the sample, or a group of sufficient size (males and females, more and less developed countries), we can predict with some accuracy the *proportion* or *percentage* of cases with specific outcomes or whether they will change, the proportion or percentage that will change in a certain way, and the *average* (mean, median, modal) amount by which they will change. We cannot predict with any certainty the outcomes for individual cases or whether, how, or by how much they will change. (This is analogous to the situation in the physical sciences with quantum mechanics; see note 3.) This is because the underlying assumption in probabilistic models is that there is some influence or set of influences on behavior that, on the individual case level, operates as a probabilistic process. Cases with certain characteristics may be more or less likely than cases with other characteristics to change in a specified way, but individual cases need not be consistent in their patterns of change with other cases in the group or sample. The Mauldin and Berelson (1978) and Tsui and Bogue (1978) models for fertility, described earlier, are examples of probabilistic models.

One way of viewing probabilistic models is to think of individuals as having various influences on their behavior (stronger influences in a particular direction for some individuals or groups, weaker influences for others) but at the same time as having some freedom to choose among different patterns of behavior and even to resist strong influences in a particular direction. Some individuals will choose to resist the measurable influences on their behavior, even if those influences are strong, but a smaller percentage of cases will resist a strong influence than will resist a weak influence (implying a smaller error of prediction for a strong influence).

In the social sciences, deterministic models are relatively rare, and when they are used, they are usually used to model quantitative variables. Probabilistic models, particularly statistical models, are much more common in the social sciences, and they are used extensively for both qualitative and quantitative variables. The remainder of this chapter will focus on statistical models used to analyze longitudinal data in the social sciences. Selecting an appropriate model to analyze a particular research question depends on a number of assumptions about the phenomena in question, how well they are measured, and the strength of the design and implementation

64

TABLE 5.2
Analytical Models and Data Structures

FEW CASES (n < 20) MANY PERIODS (t > 20)	MANY CASES (n > 100) MANY PERIODS (t > 10)
ARIMA models: covariates, transfer function models, interrupted time series models Autoregressive (AR) time series models Lagged endogenous variable (LEV) models Multivariate dynamic analysis of categorical data with optimal scaling	Continuous time event history analysis: Cox proportional hazards and parametric hazard models Multilevel growth curve models
FEW CASES (n < 20) FEW PERIODS (t < 10)	MANY CASES (n > 100) FEW PERIODS (t < 10)
Pooled cross-sectional/time-series analysis	Linear panel analysis conditional change model (lagged endogenous variable) Linear panel analysis unconditional change model (change score) Latent growth curve analysis Discrete time event history analysis Multilevel growth curve models

of the data collection, but a good place to begin in selecting a method for causal analysis of longitudinal data is to consider the number of cases (n) and the number of time periods (t). Table 5.2 offers a rough classification of methods of longitudinal data analysis along these two dimensions. Note that there is a substantial "gray area" in Table 5.2 for more than 20-100 cases (depending on the type of analysis) and for more than 10 but less than 20 time periods. In this gray area, the selection of an appropriate method of analysis is more art than science and is better guided by experience and familiarity with the methods in question than by any rule of thumb.

Pooling Cross-Sectional and Time Series Data

Pooled cross-sectional and time series data need to be understood in two distinct ways: as a data structure and as an approach to analyzing longitudinal data. As a data structure, it is illustrated in Figure 5.2, in which periods are "stacked" as though they were part of the same cross-section. Each X in the table represents an observation on a particular case at a particular time for a particular variable, with n = 1, 2, . . ., N cases, t = 1, 2, . . .,

		VARIABLE 1: X_1	VARIABLE 2: X_2	...	VARIABLE K: X_K	DEPENDENT VARIABLE: Y
TIME 1	CASE 1	X_{111}	X_{112}		X_{11K}	Y_{11}
	CASE 2	X_{211}	X_{212}		X_{21K}	Y_{21}
	.					
	.					
	CASE N	X_{N11}	X_{N12}		X_{N1K}	Y_{N1}
TIME 2	CASE 1	X_{121}	X_{122}		X_{12K}	Y_{12}
	CASE 2	X_{221}	X_{222}		X_{22K}	Y_{22}
	.					
	.					
	CASE N	X_{N21}	X_{N22}		X_{N2K}	Y_{N2}
	.					
	.					
TIME T	CASE 1	X_{1T1}	X_{1T2}		X_{1TK}	Y_{1T}
	CASE 2	X_{2T1}	X_{2T2}		X_{2TK}	Y_{2T}
	.					
	.					
	CASE N	X_{NT1}	X_{NT2}		X_{NTK}	Y_{NT}

Figure 5.2. Data Structure for Pooled Cross-Sectional/Time Series Data

T periods, and $k = 1, 2, \ldots, K$ variables (represented by the subscripts to each X). The table in Figure 5.2 has the familiar rows-as-cases, columns-as-variables structure used in spreadsheets and statistical packages, except that the cases (rows) are repeated T times. With only one dependent variable, Y, there is no need for the third subscript, but in principle there could be more than one dependent variable. It is also possible that the cases measured at each period are different, as in a repeated cross-sectional design, in which case we would refer to a pooling of cross-sections (only) rather than to a pooled cross-sectional and time series design. The repeated cross-sectional data structure is useful for analyzing aggregate historical change, at the level of the unit (country, city, etc.) *from which* cases were sampled and can be analyzed with familiar techniques such as ordinary least squares or logistic regression, but as noted earlier, it does not permit the measurement or analysis of change in the (nonaggregated) cases themselves.

When the same cases are measured repeatedly, however, as in a longitudinal panel design, the pooled cross-sectional time series (or TSCS) data structure offers the advantage of greater statistical power and greater reliability of estimation, coupled with the disadvantage that in any analysis, parameter estimation may be confounded by correlations between either or both of true scores or errors (a) *within* cases over time or (b) *between* cases measured at the same time. The TSCS data structure is the standard format for more sophisticated techniques for analyzing longitudinal data, including latent growth curve models, multilevel growth curve models, and event history analysis. All these techniques (discussed below) require substantial numbers of cases and/or periods to obtain reliable estimates of model parameters. In the worst case scenario represented by the bottom left cell in Table 5.2, however, there are few cases and few periods. In this situation, one may be limited to descriptions of case studies; even simple descriptive statistics may not be justified. At the high end of the number of cases and periods, however, it may be possible to structure the data as in Figure 5.2 and to use less sophisticated ordinary least squares (OLS) regression or similar techniques to analyze the data. Sayrs (1989) describes several models for such pooled TSCS data, the simplest of which, the *constant coefficients* model, assumes that the measurements for the predictors and the outcome are independent even though they are measured for the same case more than once (at different periods). It is unlikely, however, that the observations of the same case at one time are totally unrelated to the observations of the same case at a different time. An alternative to the constant coefficients model, which can still be estimated using OLS regression, is the least squares dummy-variable (LSDV) model. It is also possible to calculate the LSDV model assuming that the dependence is based on periods rather than cases, but the model cannot be calculated assuming linear dependence for both periods and cases because the result would be perfect collinearity. Even for the LSDV model, the number of cases and periods required to estimate the model reliably are at the upper end of the numbers represented in the lower left cell in Table 5.2.

Sayrs also describes more complex models, including generalized least squares, random coefficients, and structural equation models, but the more complex the model, the more cases or periods are required to estimate it, and the more likely the analytical approach is to be subsumed by one of the more sophisticated techniques of longitudinal analysis described below. For example, Beck et al. (1998; Beck & Katz, 1995) suggest that TSCS models in political science typically involve 10 to 100 cases measured over a span of 20 to 50 years, and for binary outcome data they recommend the use of event history analysis (specifically, a proportional odds model with dummy variables for time, thus also incorporating the important elements of the LSDV model described above). For both categorical and continuous outcomes, it is possible to construct random coefficient models (parallel to Sayrs, 1989, chap. 5) to account for both within-case clustering (i.e., multiple observations of the same case at different times) and time dependence of observations (the latter by including some function of time as a predictor, possibly interacting with other predictors in the model). As Kessler and Greenberg (1981) and Sayrs (1989) suggest, simpler methods for the analysis of TSCS data can be useful when numbers of cases and periods are small, as in the bottom left cell of Table 5.2, but when the number of cases and periods is sufficiently large, it is preferable to employ other methods.

Time Series Analysis

The top left cell of Table 5.2 represents a wealth of periods but a dearth of cases. In this situation, we are typically interested in examining patterns of change in just one case, or perhaps several cases (perhaps with some non-statistical, informal comparison across cases), and the primary interest is in generalizing across time periods rather than across cases. Technically, whenever we have data on the same variable for the same case for two or more periods, we have a time series, but the term "time series analysis" is usually reserved to describe a family of methods for analyzing relatively long time series for a single case at a time. Different types of time series analysis include Autoregressive Integrated Moving Average (ARIMA) models (Box et al., 1994; Wei, 1990; Yaffee & McGee, 2000); time series regression (TSR) models, also described by several other names including simple autoregressive or econometric time series models (Ostrom, 1990; Yaffee & McGee, 2000); lagged endogenous variable (LEV) models (Sanders & Ward, 1994); and spectral analysis, a variant of time series analysis used less frequently than the other three methods in social science data analysis (Jenkins & Watts, 1968; Wei, 1990). In addition, for qualitative dependent variables, Bijleveld et al. (1998:132-148) discuss multivariate dynamic analysis of categorical data using optimum scaling techniques, but this technique is also used relatively rarely. In the analysis of "interrupted" time series (Cook & Campbell, 1979; Wei, 1990; Yaffee & McGee, 2000), at least one dichotomous predictor representing a qualitative change in a variable believed or intended to influence the dependent variable is included in the model.

ARIMA time series analysis has become increasingly popular in the social sciences, especially since the publication of Box and Jenkins (1970). ARIMA time series analysis attempts to describe long series of time-ordered data in terms of some combination of four processes. A white noise process is a series of random shocks or changes; this is the probabilistic component that is present in all stochastic time series models. An autoregressive (AR) process is one in which the present values of a variable depend on past values of that same variable at some specified lag(s) or interval(s). A moving average (MA) process is one in which past values of the white noise process continue to influence present values of the modeled variable for some finite, specified lag(s) or interval(s). An integrated (I) process is one in which there is a detectable trend or drift over time in the values of the modeled variable but in which there is no trend or drift in the series that results from subtracting values of the variable from values of the variable at some later time. The purpose of subtracting or *differencing* is to obtain a *stationary* white noise time series, one in which the value of the white noise process has a mean of zero (that is, the value of the random component of the series at one time is uncorrelated with the value of that series at another time for any specified time interval). A time series analysis may incorporate one, two, or all three of the processes in addition to the white noise process in order to obtain a stationary time series and to describe how a variable changes over time. In addition, it is possible to incorporate continuous or categorical predictors (the latter, e.g., in interrupted time series analysis) in ARIMA models (Sanders & Ward, 1994; Wei, 1990; Yaffee & McGee, 2000).

The TSR model looks formally like an OLS regression model, except that it refers to one case instead of many and to many periods instead of one. Because the measurement of the dependent variable and the predictors are for a single case over time, however, the OLS regression assumption that the error terms are uncorrelated is usually false. The Durbin-Watson statistic is used to test for autocorrelated error, and if autocorrelated error is present, the model is reestimated using Estimated Generalized Least Squares (EGLS) or Maximum Likelihood (ML) estimation techniques in place of OLS. An autoregressive component is added to the model, parallel to the AR component in ARIMA models. Depending on the estimation methods used (ML but not EGLS for time series regression, a linear transfer function without prewhitening for ARIMA; see Yaffee & McGee, 2000, for details), it is possible to obtain identical results from ARIMA and TSR for the same model specification. It is also possible to specify a TSR model that includes a lagged endogenous variable, but then a different test for autocorrelated error (the Durbin *h* or the more general Breusch-Godfrey test; see Ostrom, 1990:65-67) and different estimation procedures are required. TSR requires fewer periods and, more important, is easier to use with a larger number of predictors than are readily accommodated in ARIMA models (Ostrom, 1990; Yaffee & McGee, 2000, chaps. 9-10). These authors and others also describe ARIMA models as being more empirically driven (the cross-correlation function determines causal order) than TSR models (the causal order is specified in advance), but it is possible using Granger causality analysis (see Chapter 2) to specify causal order empirically in TSR models.

LEV time series models use OLS regression techniques to predict the values of an outcome, Y, based on the values of a set of predictors, X_1, $X_2, \ldots, X_k$, plus one or more prior values of Y. Most often, a single lagged value of Y, Y_{t-1}, is included in the model. As noted by Sanders and Ward (1994:203) the two advantages to the LEV model are that it frequently avoids the problem of serially correlated error associated with the use of OLS regression without a lagged endogenous variable, and the lagged value(s) of Y can incorporate all the past effects of unmeasured variables on the current value of Y. It is still possible, however, that errors will be serially correlated or autocorrelated (i.e., the error at one time will be correlated with the error at another time) and that the effects of the predictors on the outcome may not be stable over time.

TSR time series test and correct for serially correlated error and thus represent an improvement over the LEV model. ARIMA models account not only for serially correlated error but also for trend or drift (the integrated or I component) by differencing the series one or more times and for period-specific random shocks (the moving average or MA component). So why even consider the LEV or TSR models? Because the more complex the model, the more demands it makes on the number of periods needed for reliable model estimation. The ARIMA model, as previously noted, may require as many as 250 periods, while the LEV model can, in principle, be estimated with far fewer periods. In practice, ARIMA models are most often used for purely descriptive or very simple (one or two predictors) models of change. TSR and LEV models are more often used when a larger number of predictors and fewer periods are involved. All of these methods are typically used to model quantitative dependent variables. In principle, all three could be adapted to analyze qualitative dependent variables, but in practice this would be easier with LEV models (just replace OLS linear regression with ML logistic regression or similar techniques).

Time series analysis has long been used in economic analysis and forecasting, and Vigderhous (1977) applied it to the study of suicide. Sanders and Ward (1994) compared OLS regression, ARIMA, TSR (which they designated AR), and LEV models to analyze the impact of economic conditions, consumer confidence, and the Falklands War on British voting patterns. The OLS model was unsatisfactory because, as expected, there was evidence of high autocorrelation of the errors. Importantly, the three other models led to different substantive conclusions. All three found a significant autoregressive effect (dependence on prior values or inertia, which Sanders and Ward interpreted as an inclination to support the government), and all three found a significant effect of consumer confidence on voting preferences. Only the LEV model indicated a significant impact of economic conditions on voter preference, and only the TSR model failed to find any longer term impact of the Falklands War. Asking how to choose among the three models, Sanders and Ward (1994:218) concluded, "There is, sadly, no easy or general answer to the question." For epistemological reasons (the LEV process seemed to more closely parallel the decision-making process of individual voters), they preferred the LEV model in this specific instance, but hastened to add that this did not imply that the LEV technique is always the best model for time series analysis.

Methods for Short Time Series With Many Cases

The bottom right cell in Table 5.2 represents what is probably the most frequent situation for longitudinal analysis in the social sciences: a large sample or population of cases but few periods, the opposite of the problem we faced in the previous section. For quantitative data, but increasingly expanding to include qualitative data as well, structural equation modeling (SEM) techniques are used for the causal analysis of differences and change in linear panel analysis and for the description and explanation of change in latent growth curve models. Stage-state models focus on probabilities of transitions among discrete, qualitative states, and include Markov chains and loglinear models. All these models, for practical reasons, have been largely limited to analysis of short time series. Event history analysis and multilevel growth curve models, also represented in the bottom right cell in Table 5.2, are more flexible and will be discussed later in connection with the top right cell in Table 5.2.

Linear Panel Analysis. Linear panel analysis (Finkel, 1995; Kessler & Greenberg, 1981; Markus, 1979) was described in Chapter 2 ("Temporal Order of Measurement, Causal Order, and Linear Panel Analysis") in the context of ascertaining causal order. It may be used with as few as two periods, is often used with three, and is rarely used for data involving more than five periods. Linear panel analysis can, in principle, be used to analyze any of the basic models (A, B, C, D) presented earlier, but most commonly it is used to analyze either model A, the *conditional change model*, or model D, the *unconditional change model* (Finkel, 1995). The conditional change model is similar to the lagged endogenous variable (LEV) time series model described in the previous section, except that usually only the immediately prior value of Y is included as a predictor. In the unconditional change model, we have the change in Y, $(Y_t - Y_{t-1})$, as the dependent variable and changes in $X_1, X_2, \ldots, X_k$ as predictors, that is, $(X_{1,t} - X_{1,t-1})$, $(X_{2,t} - X_{2,t-1}), \ldots, (X_{k,t} - X_{k,t-1})$ are on the right side of the equation. The linear panel model can be used to analyze experimental or quasi-experimental data, in which case at least one of the predictors is the presence or absence of a treatment or intervention, the other predictors are covariates (other predictors thought to affect the outcome of the treatment or intervention), and the preferred method of analysis is OLS linear regression, analysis of variance, or analysis of covariance. In this type of research, the most common pattern is to have two measurement periods for Y and its predictors, one before and one after treatment, and to be more concerned with the magnitude and direction of change in Y than in the actual value of Y at the end of the treatment. Alternatively, the model can be used to analyze nonexperimental data, most often using structural equation modeling (Bollen, 1989; Hayduk, 1987; Kaplan, 2000), frequently with more than two periods and often with less of a focus on the change in Y than on differences in the value of Y for cases with different values of the predictors.

Change Score Versus Lagged Endogenous Variable Models. There has been disagreement in the social and behavioral sciences about the appropriateness of change scores ($Y_t - Y_{t-1}$) as measures of change when the purpose is to analyze change in panels with short time series data. *It is important to emphasize that this debate is relevant primarily to the analysis of short-term intraindividual change.* For longer series of data, when the concern shifts from the magnitude of short-term change to the pattern of longer term change, the issue largely disappears (Bijleveld et al., 1998:39; Raudenbush & Bryk, 2002:166-167). Cronbach and Furby (1970) argued against the use of change scores because change scores are systematically related to any random error of measurement, are typically less reliable than the scores of the variables (e.g., X_1 and X_2) from which they are calculated, and the unreliability of change scores may lead to fallacious conclusions or false inferences. They also argued against the use of residual gain scores as change variables (for similar reasons) and suggested that residual gain scores be used only (as a more appropriate alternative to change scores for this purpose) to identify cases that changed more or less than expected based on their initial scores. Plewis (1985) concurred and observed that the problem of measurement error is just as serious for residual gain scores as for change scores. The model recommended by these and other authors is the conditional change model (Finkel, 1995; Kessler & Greenberg, 1981), which includes the lagged endogenous variable Y_{t-1}.

Authors who have argued in favor of using change scores, at least under certain circumstances (Allison, 1990; Liker et al., 1985; Rogosa, 1995; Stoolmiller & Bank, 1995) have done so in the context of the unconditional change model, based on the assumptions that we are interested in explaining intraindividual change rather than in causal analysis of differences; that our time series is short (most typically only two, or perhaps three, periods); and that certain other assumptions are met. Liker et al. (1985) demonstrated that the unconditional change model may be superior to both cross-sectional equations and the conditional change model when (a) regression parameters remain constant from one period to another, (b) there are unmeasured variables that influence the dependent variable but do not change over time, (c) there is autocorrelated error in the measurement of those variables which both influence the dependent variable and vary over time, and (d) the panel data give more reliable measurement of *changes* in predictor variables over time than of the level or value of predictor variables at any given time, as may be the case if interindividual differences in change are large relative to interindividual differences in initial scores (see also Rogosa, 1995; Stoolmiller & Bank, 1995). These conditions under which the unconditional change model is preferable to the lagged endogenous variable model are quite restrictive, unlikely to be met in most observational research, and difficult to meet even in experimental or quasi-experimental research (Cronbach & Furby, 1970; Finkel, 1995). Stoolmiller and Bank (1995) acknowledge that when interindividual differences in change are small, the conditional change model may be more useful.

Allison (1990) also defends the use of the unconditional change model for the study of intraindividual change in the context of the quasi-experimental nonequivalent control group design. Assuming stable group differences (i.e., different "types" of cases, parallel to criterion *b* as described by Liker et al., 1985) in the absence of any treatment, and also assuming no interaction between the treatment and the pretest score, Y_{t-1}, the unconditional change model appears to work better than the conditional change model. Allison notes, however, that when there is an interaction between the treatment and the initial value of Y (e.g., when individuals are selected for a math tutoring program based on low scores on a math achievement test), the conditional change model may be preferable to the unconditional change model. In addition, the conditional change model may be more appropriate when there is a true causal effect of Y_{t-1} on Y_t. This raises a conceptual issue that is sometimes ignored in discussions of the relative advantages of conditional versus unconditional change models: social inertia. As Davies (1994:33) explains, "Positive temporal dependence, or inertia, is to be expected of most social behaviour." McGinnis (1968:716) suggested the axiom that "the probability of remaining in any state of nature increases as a strict monotone function of prior residence in that state." Finkel (1995:7) notes that the prior value of Y may influence the current value of Y, and the influence of Y_{t-1} on Y_t may be misspecified by an unconditional change model.

The coefficient of the lagged endogenous variable is sometimes called the "stability coefficient." There are several interpretations of the stability coefficient that are statistically indistinguishable; which interpretation is most appropriate must be decided based on conceptual or theoretical considerations (Davies, 1994; Finkel, 1995; Kessler & Greenberg, 1981;

Rogosa, 1995). Most commonly, it is interpreted either as a control for prior, unmeasured influences on Y or as the inertial effect of past values of Y on the present value of Y. Alternatively, it may be interpreted as doing several things at once. Davies (1994) indicates that the stability coefficient may represent the impact of a previous state or behavior on a present state or behavior, plus prior impacts of measured variables, plus effects of unmeasured variables, on the dependent variable Y_t. In short, the conditional change model provides a liberal estimate of inertial effects and a conservative estimate of the effects of other predictors in the model. In this respect, as Davies (1994:36-37) notes, the conditional change model is far from perfect; it tends to overestimate the inertial effect and underestimate the influence of other predictors of Y_t. In light of the observation (Davies, 1994:32) that the impact of interventions is often less than that predicted by statistical models, this characteristic may actually be an advantage for the conditional change model.

Latent Growth Curve Models. In linear panel models, the focus is often first on predicting or explaining differences between cases in the values of one or more dependent variables and only secondarily on describing the pattern of change. In latent growth curve models (Bijleveld et al., 1998, chap. 4; Kaplan, 2000, chap. 8; McArdle & Bell, 2000; Stoolmiller, 1995), this order of priorities is reversed, and the description or analysis of change is paramount. Adapting the simplified notation from Bijleveld et al. (1998:250), the latent growth curve model without covariates can be written as $\hat{Y}_t = Z_1 + Z_2 t$, where $\hat{Y}_t$ is the observed value of Y at time t, $t = 0, 1, 2,$ . . ., T; t is the index of time (or age); Z_1 is a latent variable parameter representing the Y-intercept or the initial value (at $t = 0$) of Y; and Z_2 is a latent variable parameter representing the growth rate or slope of the growth curve indicated by the pattern of values of Y over time. In this equation, Z_1 has taken the place of the usual Y-intercept, the fixed parameter α, and Z_2 replaces the usual fixed parameter β as the slope of the growth curve (the coefficient of time). Covariates may be added to the model to explain either the dependent variable Y or the parameters of the latent growth curve, Z_1 and Z_2; if the latter, the structure of the model parallels the usual structure of the multilevel growth curve model, to be discussed later. There are details excluded from the above equation, including any measurement model for the dependent variable or the predictors and the model for any correlations among errors. A fully detailed model, however, might prove a bit unwieldy in the present context. For example, Stoolmiller (1995) used 27 equations to provide a detailed specification of a single 4-period latent growth curve model for intelligence. Several examples of latent growth curve models for a variety of dependent variables, including cognitive performance, mental health, alcohol and illicit drug use, and other illegal and deviant behavior, can be found in Little et al. (2000) and Collins and Sayer (2001).

In both textbook treatments and empirical research applications of SEM latent growth curve models, the number of periods is typically 2 to 7, and it seems that 4 or 5 waves of data is the modal pattern (see, e.g., chapters involving SEM latent growth curve models in Collins & Sayer, 2001; Gottman, 1995; and Little et al., 2000). In these short time series models, latent growth curve models generally produce results identical or very similar to the results obtained using multilevel growth curve models (Little et al., 2000). As a practical matter, the ideal situation for the use of latent growth curve models would involve five or fewer variables, all unmeasured and in principle unmeasurable, for each of which an internal consistency measure of reliability is appropriate, with three to five indicators for each variable, and a potentially complex covariance structure, possibly including correlated errors. More variables or more indicators would require increasingly large sample sizes or more constraints on the model (which would need to be theoretically justified). Bijleveld et al. (1998:267) suggest that "in general, one may state that structural equation models are suitable when a theoretical model with a high degree of specificity needs to be tested, in which a large number of subjects have been measured on a small number of occasions." They continue by observing that fitting structural equation models to a large number of time points "may become increasingly complicated or even arrive at improper solutions when the number of subjects becomes too small for the complexity of the problem at hand." Bijleveld et al. recommend fitting small parts of the model and assembling the results until satisfactory results are obtained, and their general discussion (pp. 265-268) offers sensible advice for the practical application of structural equation models to longitudinal data.

Descriptive Models of Qualitative Change: Stage-State Analysis and Transition Matrices. Models of change for qualitative data often use stage-state analyses, classifications into finite sets of categories such that a case may move from one category to another over time. Stage-state models of change are concerned with the probability of moving from one value (state) to another value of a variable by a given period (stage). For multiple category or *multivalent* categorical variables, separate probabilities of *transition* (movement from one value to another in a given interval between periods) are calculated for each pair of *origin* (the state or value at the beginning of the interval) and *destination* (the state or value at the end of the interval) states, including those instances when the origin state is the same as the destination state. When the origin and the destination are one and the same, the transition probability indicates the stability of membership in that state over the specified interval.

Stage-state models of change in the social sciences are characteristically probabilistic, not deterministic. Stage-state transitions may be described using simple transition matrices, with no assumptions about underlying properties of the transition matrices (e.g., Elliott et al., 1989:179); Markov models, including Markov chains (Bartholomew, 1973; Bijleveld et al., 1998, chap. 6); loglinear models (Bijleveld et al., 1998, chap. 6; Hout, 1983); latent variable approaches, including mixed Markov latent class models and latent transition analysis (Collins, 2001; Collins et al., 2000; Langeheine & van de Pol, 1994); life table models (Namboodiri & Suchindran, 1987); or survival, hazard, or event history analysis models (Allison, 1984; Blossfeld et al., 1989; Hosmer & Lemeshow, 1999; Yamaguchi, 1991). Transition matrices, including those involving Markov models and loglinear models, are based on simple row percentages from cross-tabulations or contingency tables that compare the values of a variable at one time (the column variable) with the values of that same variable at a later time (the row variable) for the same set of cases. In some Markov models, there exist *absorbing states,* which, once entered, cannot be left. The most common example of an absorbing state is death. For homogeneous Markov processes with at least one absorbing state, every case will eventually enter an absorbing state, and it is possible to calculate (a) what proportion of cases will be in the absorbing state(s), and each other state, at a given period, and (b) how long it will take all cases, or a certain proportion of cases, to enter the absorbing state(s).

Elliott et al. (1989) used transition matrices to model transitions from nondelinquency to increasing levels of delinquency and drug use in adolescence. They used five stages (1976-1980) and four states (nonoffenders, exploratory offenders, patterned nonserious offenders, and serious offenders for delinquency; nonusers, alcohol users, marijuana users, and polydrug users for drug use). Transition matrices for delinquency were *homogeneous*; they varied from one period to another no more than would be expected based on random error, according to a chi-square test described in Markus (1979). The delinquency matrices for adolescence approximated a stationary Markov process. For drug use, the transition matrices were statistically significantly different from one period to the next, or *nonhomogeneous*, primarily because patterns of transition to higher levels of drug use become more likely in later adolescence than they are in earlier adolescence. Elliott et al. used these transition matrices as part of a larger analysis to describe developmental patterns in illegal behavior. They also used transition matrices to examine the onset or initiation and the suspension of different types of illegal behavior.

Methods for Long Time Series With Many Cases

The top right cell of Table 5.2 would seem to represent the longitudinal researcher's dream: many cases measured at many periods. (Actually, not so many periods, from the perspective of ARIMA models, but many for most other statistical techniques.) Yet only two analytical methods are listed in this cell of the table: continuous time event history analysis and multi-level growth curve models, both of which are also listed in the lower right cell (many cases, few periods). As noted by several authors cited in the previous section, other techniques such as linear panel analysis, latent growth curve analysis, stage-state models, and even ANOVA, ANCOVA, MANOVA (multivariate analysis of variance), and MANCOVA (multivariate analysis of covariance) models have difficulty with long time series data. Event history analysis and multilevel growth curve models, in contrast, are flexible techniques that are easily adapted to longer or shorter time series.

Event History Analysis. Event history analysis (Blossfeld et al., 1989; Hosmer & Lemeshow, 1999; Namboodiri & Suchindran, 1987; Yamaguchi, 1991), which includes survival and hazard analysis, is a family of methods that links regression analysis and the analysis of transition matrices for data that include measurements at several periods. In event history analysis, the primary concern is with describing, predicting, and explaining the *timing* of qualitative change. Event history analysis allows the use of either age or chronological time as the underlying time continuum and the use of the other time variable as an independent variable so that both historical and developmental trends may be examined. Life table models, including multistate life table models, may in a sense be regarded as a nonparametric form of event history analysis. They analyze stage-state transitions without making any assumptions about the underlying temporal distribution of those transitions (as in event history analysis) and in that sense are more flexible than event history analysis, but they also have greater difficulty handling large numbers of independent variables.

For short time series, *discrete time* (alternatively described by some authors as *grouped time*, *grouped duration*, or *interval censored*; see Beck et al., 1998, and Hosmer & Lemeshow, 1999:257-269) *event history analysis* models require only a few (often four or five) periods, and can be estimated using logistic regression (for proportional odds) or complementary log-log models (for proportional hazards). The short time series may result from events really occurring at discrete intervals (one can vote for a Republican, Democrat, or Independent candidate for president of the United States only once every 4 years) or from crude measurement of time (e.g., long measurement intervals, resulting in measurement only once per year for events that may occur at any time during the year). For longer series, typically but not necessarily involving more precise measurement of time, either the semiparametric *Cox proportional hazards* model or the *parametric* event history analysis model may be used. (Note that the Cox proportional hazards model is only one version of the proportional hazards model; some parametric and discrete time models are also proportional hazards models.) Event history analysis has been used in both descriptive analysis and causal analysis, for example, to model recidivism (Schmidt & Witte, 1988), labor force participation (Blossfeld et al., 1989), marital history events (Peters, 1988), and other events that involve transitions among discrete states.

Multilevel Growth Curve Models and Related Methods. Multilevel growth curve models of intraindividual (or more generally intracase) change are discussed in Bijleveld et al. (1998, chap. 5), Raudenbush and Bryk (2002, chap. 6), and Snijders and Bosker (1999, chap. 12). Raudenbush et al. (2000) and Snijders and Bosker (1999) include chapters on analysis of categorical (dichotomous, nominal, ordinal, and count) dependent variables. The basic model for multilevel analysis of longitudinal data involves two levels, the individual or case level (level 2), with data that describe characteristics of the case that do not vary over time, and the observation level (level 1), with data on repeated measurements of individual characteristics, including the dependent variable, that do vary over time. A simple descriptive growth curve model would include no level 2 predictors and only a measure of time or age (or both) as a predictor (e.g., X_1 = time) in the level 1 model. In this case the effect of time on the dependent variable is said to be fixed (as opposed to random, i.e., variable). More complex models could include more complex functions of time (e.g., quadratic or cubic polynomials) and additional time-invariant covariates at level 2 plus time-varying covariates at level 1. Put together, these two levels can examine the impact of stable individual characteristics (level 2) on not only the dependent variable but also on the relationship between the dependent variable and time and between the dependent variable and the other level 1 predictors over time. This includes the possibility of examining whether and how different individual characteristics affect whether and how the relationship between a predictor and the dependent variable changes with age or time; in other words, whether the slope of the growth curve is affected by the characteristics of the individual case, including both stable characteristics and time-varying characteristics of that case.

Bijleveld et al. (1998, chap. 3) also discuss the use of repeated measures univariate analysis of variance (ANOVA) and covariance (ANCOVA) and multivariate analysis of variance (MANOVA) and covariance (MANCOVA), for the analysis of longitudinal data and (chap. 5) provide a useful comparison with multilevel models. As a practical matter, repeated measures

ANOVA, ANCOVA, MANOVA, and MANCOVA are subsets of multilevel mixed models (including the multilevel growth curve model), the latter of which are generally better suited to the analysis of longitudinal data with more than two or three periods. Repeated measures ANOVA, ANCOVA, MANOVA, and MANCOVA are most useful in the analysis of very short series of quantitative data, particularly series with only two or three time periods, as are frequently encountered in experimental and quasi-experimental research. Multilevel growth curve models are more flexible and can be as easily adapted to the analysis of qualitative as quantitative dependent variables. Unlike latent growth curve models, they can easily handle long time series (large numbers of periods), and in fact the reliability of multilevel growth curve models improves as the number of periods increases. They can also handle series as short as those typically modeled using latent growth curve models, and when the two methods are compared for these shorter series of data, the results tend to be similar (Little et al., 2000). Raudenbush and Bryk (2002) illustrate the use of multilevel growth curves for modeling cognitive growth and vocabulary acquisition. Raudenbush (1995) uses National Youth Survey data and multilevel growth curve modeling to examine the relationship over the life course in attitudes toward deviance, exposure to delinquent friends, age, and sex and also (Raudenbush, 2001) to analyze a dichotomous dependent variable, the probability of committing a serious theft, longitudinally for ages 11 to 21.

Conclusion: Longitudinal Versus
Cross-Sectional Data and Analysis

This monograph began by contrasting pure cross-sectional research with longitudinal research and did so for the purpose of defining longitudinal research. It ends now by summarizing the differences between the two.

1. Longitudinal research typically costs more. If the research question or hypothesis can be addressed satisfactorily with cross-sectional data, there is little or no point in trying to use longitudinal research to answer the research question or test the hypothesis.

2. Longitudinal research has the same problems and issues of data quality and adequacy of sampling as cross-sectional research, and a few more besides. There are ways of addressing these issues, but again if cross-sectional research is adequate to the task, it is to be preferred over longitudinal research.

3. Cross-sectional research cannot disentangle developmental (age) trends, historical (period) trends, and cohort effects. Whenever all three types of effects are possible, the study of any or all of these three types of change requires longitudinal data.

4. The description and analysis of historical change absolutely requires the use of longitudinal data; also, longitudinal methods of analysis such as differential equation models (in which differentiation is performed with respect to time), ARIMA time series models, and event history analysis may provide more powerful and detailed analyses of historical change than would those methods common to both longitudinal and cross-sectional analysis.

5. The description and analysis of developmental trends may be attempted with cross-sectional age-specific (or stage-specific) data, but the results will not necessarily reflect those obtained by using longitudinal data. Insofar as developmental change is conceived as reflecting the experience of individuals as they age or pass through successive stages, longitudinal data, because they reflect intraindividual change rather than interindividual differences, are to be preferred.

6. Unless there is good reason to believe otherwise (e.g., unless it is known that a dynamic process is nonergodic), it should be assumed that longitudinal data are necessary to estimate the parameters, efficiently and without bias, of any dynamic process in the social sciences.

7. Unless recall periods are short, or problems of respondent conditioning are severe, or unless it can be demonstrated that problems of long-term recall are minor or nonexistent, prospective panel designs or total population designs are generally to be preferred over other longitudinal designs.

8. Testing for temporal or causal order should be an integral component in testing causal hypotheses. Along with covariation (as indicated by the strength of the relationship) and nonspuriousness (as indicated by the continued significance of the relationship when the effects of other variables are considered), temporal or causal order, as indicated in stage-state temporal order analysis, Granger causality, or linear panel analysis, is a crucial element in any causal relationship.

In light of these conclusions, what role remains to cross-sectional research? The most readily apparent answer is that cross-sectional research remains important for describing variables and patterns of relationships as they exist at a particular time. Cross-sectional research must also be considered as a relatively less expensive alternative to longitudinal research for those instances in which cross-sectional research is demonstrably adequate and for exploratory or preliminary investigation of hypotheses or research questions that involve dynamic models. If the concern is with differences between individuals of different ages at one time, and not with inferring intraindividual changes that occur with age over the life course, cross-sectional research is again preferable. The conclusion is inescapable, however, that for the description and analysis of dynamic change processes, longitudinal research is ultimately indispensable. It is also the case that longitudinal research can, in principle, do much that cross-sectional research cannot but that there is little or nothing that cross-sectional research can, in principle, do that longitudinal research cannot.

Longitudinal research is not the cure for all the problems of cross-sectional research. It cannot cure problems of poor research design (quite the contrary—it is likely to magnify such problems), inadequate sampling, or failure to pay attention to the assumptions and limitations of analytical techniques. Longitudinal research is not an absolute necessity for all research problems; there is much that has been done and much that can be accomplished with cross-sectional research. Longitudinal research is best viewed as a powerful tool but only one of several that are available to the social scientist. If the research question does not require longitudinal research, then its use would be a waste of time, money, and effort. If the research question or hypothesis does require longitudinal data and analysis, then the costs of longitudinal research, if longitudinal research is used well, are likely to be amply compensated by the quality of the results.

NOTES

1. For a discussion of the use of social indicators and a presentation of some indicators of social change, see Bauer (1966) and Sheldon and Moore (1968). The U.S. Bureau of the Census (1975) presents statistics on the United States from colonial times up to 1970, and Caplow et al. (2001) present trends in a wide array of social indicators for the United States during the 20th century.

2. For basic discussions of causal modeling, see Asher (1983), Blalock (1964), Davis (1985), Heise (1975), and Pearl (2000). For an approach from the philosophy of science, see Nagel (1961). Recent debates about drawing causal inferences from nonexperimental research may be found in Marsden (1991, chaps. 10-14), McKim and Turner (1997) and Shaffer (1992), most of them limited to modeling intraindividual change (not in the causal analysis of differences between individuals) for data involving few periods or cross-sectional designs. Drawing causal inferences from nonexperimental research in the "hard" sciences (astronomy is a good example) tends to be either ignored or glossed over, in arguments that suggest requiring an "as if by experiment" standard (implying random assignment to treatment and manipulation of the putative causal variable) for the social sciences. Briefly, in my view, both experimental and non-experimental research offer *evidence*, not *proof*, about causal relationships, and both have inherent limitations (Babbie, 2001:226-235; Campbell & Stanley, 1963; Cook & Campbell, 1979) plus potential limitations imposed by poor implementation. Although experimental research clearly has an advantage over nonexperimental research, that advantage is a matter of degree, not kind.

3. One might suggest additional criteria as well. For instance, one might insist on some mechanism or linkage that connects cause with effect. This is a rather vague criterion, and in the social sciences may suggest no more than a set of intervening variables. In the physical sciences, it may consist of a rejection in principle of "action at a distance"; that is for one mass/energy cluster to affect another mass/energy cluster, there must be some contact, some exchange of a particle or wave; but quantum theory apparently implies the existence of action at a distance. Thomsen (1987) writes that "quantum mechanical causality is statistical, and it applies to large ensembles of individuals. Its probabilities are usually between 0 and 1, and the customary interpretation of them is that a certain fraction of the individuals will do one thing and a certain fraction something else" (p. 346). This description of causality, along with the assertion that "quantum mechanics cannot make predictions about individual objects" (p. 346), is consistent with the idea of causality as it is used in the social sciences, and the allowance of action at a distance would seem to eliminate the need for a fourth criterion of causality (mechanism or linkage). For a more extended treatment of the topic of causality, see Babbie (2001, chap. 3), Blalock (1964, 1971), Cook and Campbell (1979, chaps. 1, 4), and Nagel (1961). For a dissenting view that suggests that the term *causality* is improperly used and unnecessary for investigation in the social sciences, see Kerlinger (1986:361).

4. The National Crime Survey (NCS) was later renamed the National Crime Victimization Survey (NCVS), but for consistency with the terminology used in studies of the survey methodology, the earlier designation is used throughout this monograph except where the NCS and NCVS are compared.

5. If N is the number of cases across all periods and T is the number of periods for which data are available for the cases, then if $N(T-1)$ cases would be sufficient to allow the use of a particular method (e.g., tests for the statistical significance of differences in means, or multiple regression with three or four independent variables), it may be appropriate to pool the cross-sectional and time-series data into a single two- or three-wave longitudinal analysis.

6. Taris (2000, chap. 2) provides good introductory coverage of approaches to dealing with missing data in longitudinal research. Allison (2002) and Rovine and Delaney (1990) offer similar coverage at a more advanced level. Kasprzyk et al. (1989, Part VII) and Little et al. (2000, especially chaps. 10-12 and 14) devote several chapters to the issue of missing data in longitudinal research. Lepkowski (1989) compares weighting and imputation methods to adjust for respondent loss, including loss at an earlier wave followed by participation at a later wave, cross-wave as well as within-wave imputation, and approaches for combining imputation and weighting to deal with missing data.

REFERENCES

AGRESTI, A., & FINLAY, B. (1997). *Statistical methods for the social sciences* (3rd ed.). Upper Saddle River, NJ: Prentice Hall.

AHLUWALIA, M. S. (1974). Income inequality: Some dimensions of the problem. In H. B. Chenery, M. S. Ahluwalia, C. L. G. Bell, J. H. Duloy, & R. Jolly (Eds.), *Redistribution with growth: An approach to policy* (pp. 3-37). Oxford, UK: Oxford University Press.

AHLUWALIA, M. S. (1976). Inequality, poverty, and development. *Journal of Development Economics, 2,* 307-342.

ALLISON, P. D. (1984). *Event history analysis: Regression for longitudinal event data.* Beverly Hills, CA: Sage.

ALLISON, P. D. (1990). Change scores as dependent variables in regression analysis. In C. C. Clogg (Ed.), *Sociological methodology 1990* (Vol. 20, pp. 93-114). Washington, DC: American Sociological Association.

ALLISON, P. D. (2002). *Missing data.* Thousand Oaks, CA: Sage.

APPLEMAN, P. (Ed.). (1976). *Thomas Robert Malthus: An essay on the principle of population.* New York: Norton.

ARMAS, G. C. (2001, March 2.). "Battle brewing over census count." Associated Press.

ASHER, H. B. (1983). *Causal modeling* (2nd ed.). Thousand Oaks, CA: Sage.

BABBIE, E. (2001). *The practice of social research* (9th ed.). Belmont, CA: Wadsworth.

BALTES, P. B., CORNELIUS, S. W., & NESSELROADE, J. R. (1979). Cohort effects in developmental psychology. In J. R. Nesselroade & P. B. Baltes (Eds.), *Longitudinal research in the study of behavior and development* (pp. 61-87). New York: Academic Press.

BALTES, P. B., & NESSELROADE, J. R. (1979). History and rationale of longitudinal research. In J. R. Nesselroade & P. B. Baltes (Eds.), *Longitudinal research in the study of behavior and development* (pp. 1-39). New York: Academic Press.

BARNARD, J. R., & KRAUTMANN, A. C. (1988). Population growth among U.S. regions and metropolitan areas: A test for causality. *Journal of Regional Science, 22,* 103-118.

BARTHOLOMEW, D. J. (1973). *Stochastic models for social processes* (2nd ed.). New York: John Wiley.

BAUER, R. A. (Ed.). (1966). *Social indicators.* Cambridge: MIT Press.

BECK, N., & KATZ, J. N. (1995). What to do (and not to do) with time-series cross-section data. *American Political Science Review, 82,* 634-647.

BECK, N., KATZ, J. N., & TUCKER, R. (1998). Taking time seriously: Time-series-cross-section analysis with a binary dependent variable. *American Journal of Political Science, 42,* 1260-1288.

BECKER, G. S., LANDES, E. M., & MICHAEL, F. T. (1977). An economic analysis of marital instability. *Journal of Political Economy, 82,* 1141-1187.

BERRUETA-CLEMENT, J., SCHWEINHART, L. J., BARNETT, W. S., EPSTEIN, A. S., & WEIKART, D. P. (1984). *Changed lives: The effects of the Perry Preschool Program on youths through age 19.* Ypsilanti, MI: High/Scope Educational Research Foundation.

BERRY, W. D. (1984). *Nonrecursive causal models.* Beverly Hills, CA: Sage.

BICKMAN, L., & ROG, D. J. (Eds.). (1998). *Handbook of applied social research methods.* Thousand Oaks, CA: Sage.

BIJLEVELD, C. J. H., & VAN DER KAMP, L. J. T., with MOOIJAART, A., VAN DER KLOOT, W. A., VAN DER LEEDEN, R., & VAN DER BURG, E. (1998). *Longitudinal data analysis: Designs, models, and methods.* London: Sage.

84

BLACK, C. E. (1966). *The dynamics of modernization*. New York: Harper & Row.

BLALOCK, A. B., & BLALOCK, H. M., Jr. (1982). *An introduction to social research*. Englewood Cliffs, NJ: Prentice Hall.

BLALOCK, H. M., Jr. (1962). Four-variable causal models and partial correlations. *American Journal of Sociology, 62,* 182-194.

BLALOCK, H. M., Jr. (1964). *Causal inference in nonexperimental research*. New York: Norton.

BLALOCK, H. M., Jr. (1969). *Theory construction: From verbal to mathematical formulations*. Englewood Cliffs, NJ: Prentice Hall.

BLALOCK, H. M., Jr. (Ed.). (1971). *Causal models in the social sciences*. Chicago: Aldine.

BLAU, P. M., & DUNCAN, O. D. (1966). *The American occupational structure*. New York: John Wiley.

BLOSSFELD, H., HAMERLE, A., & MAYER, K. U. (1989). *Event history analysis: Statistical theory and application in the social sciences*. Hillsdale, NJ: Lawrence Erlbaum.

BLUMSTEIN, A., COHEN, J., ROTH, J. A., & VISHER, C. A. (Eds.). (1986). *Criminal careers and "career criminals"* (Vols. 1, 2). Washington, DC: National Academy Press.

BOLLEN, K. A. (1989). *Structural equations with latent variables*. New York: John Wiley.

BOHRNSTEDT, G. W. (1983). Measurement. In P. H. Rossi, J. D. Wright, & A. B. Anderson (Eds.), *Handbook of survey research* (pp. 69-121). Orlando, FL: Academic Press.

BOX, G. E. P., & JENKINS, G. M. (1970). *Time series analysis: Forecasting and control*. San Francisco: Holden-Day.

BOX, G. E. P., JENKINS, G. M., & REINSEL, G. C. (1994). *Time series analysis: Forecasting and control* (3rd ed.). San Francisco: Holden-Day.

BREHM, J. (1993). *The phantom respondents: Opinion surveys and political representation*. Ann Arbor: University of Michigan Press.

BROWN, C., DUNCAN, G. J., & STAFFORD, F. P. (1996). Data watch: The Panel Study of Income Dynamics. *Journal of Economic Perspectives, 12,* 155-168.

BRYK, A., & RAUDENBUSH, S. (1992). *Hierarchical linear models: Applications and data analysis methods*. Newbury Park, CA: Sage.

BULMER, M. G. (1979). *Principles of statistics*. New York: Dover.

BUREAU OF JUSTICE STATISTICS. (1992). *Criminal victimization in the United States: 1973-90 trends*. Washington, DC: U.S. Department of Justice.

BURGESS, R. D. (1989). Major issues and implications of tracing survey respondents. In D. Kasprzyk, G. Duncan, G. Kalton, & M. P. Singh (Eds.), *Panel surveys* (pp. 52-74). New York: John Wiley.

CALDWELL, J. C. (1976). Toward a restatement of demographic transition theory. *Population and Development Review, 2,* 321-366.

CAMPBELL, D. T., & STANLEY, J. C. (1963). *Experimental and quasi-experimental designs for research*. Chicago: Rand McNally.

CANTOR, D. (1989). Substantive implications of longitudinal design features: The National Crime Survey as a case study. In D. Kasprzyk, G. Duncan, G. Kalton, & M. P. Singh (Eds.), *Panel surveys* (pp. 25-51). New York: John Wiley.

CAPLOW, T., HICKS, L., & WATTENBERG, B. J. (2001). *The first measured century: An illustrated guide to trends in America, 1900-2000*. Washington, DC: AEI Press.

CARLSON, E. (1979). Divorce rate fluctuation as a cohort phenomenon. *Population Studies, 32,* 523-536.

CHILTON, R., & SPIELBERGER, A. (1971). Is delinquency increasing? Age structure and the crime rate. *Social Forces, 42,* 487-493.

CLARRIDGE, B. R., SHEEHY, L. L., & HAUSER, T. (1977). Tracing members of a panel: A 17-year follow-up. In K. F. Schuessler (Ed.), *Sociological methodology 1978* (pp. 185-203). San Francisco: Jossey-Bass.

COLLINS, C., GIVEN, B., & BERRY, D. (1989). Longitudinal studies as intervention. *Nursing Research, 32,* 251-253.

COLLINS, L. (2001). Reliability for static and dynamic categorical latent variables: developing measurement instruments based on a model of the growth process. In L. M. Collins & A. G. Sayer (Eds.), *New methods for the analysis of change* (pp. 273-288). Washington, DC: American Psychological Association.

COLLINS, L. M., HYATT, S. S., & GRAHAM, J. W. (2000). Latent transition analysis as a way of testing models of stage-sequential change in longitudinal data. In T. D. Little, K. U. Schnabel, & J. Baumert (Eds.), *Modeling longitudinal and multilevel data: Practical issues, applied approaches, and specific examples* (pp. 147-161). Mahwah, NJ: Lawrence Erlbaum.

COLLINS, L. M., & SAYER, A. G. (Eds.). (2001). *New methods for the analysis of change.* Washington, DC: American Psychological Association.

CONVERSE, J. M., & PRESSER, S. (1986). *Survey questions: Handcrafting the standardized questionnaire.* Beverly Hills, CA: Sage.

COOK, T. D., & CAMPBELL, D. T. (1979). *Quasi-experimentation: Design and analysis issues for field settings.* Chicago: Rand McNally.

CORDRAY, S., & POLK, K. (1983). The implications of respondent loss in panel studies of deviant behavior. *Journal of Research in Crime and Delinquency, 22,* 214-242.

COVEY, H. C., & MENARD, S. (1987). Trends in arrests among the elderly. *The Gerontologist, 22,* 666-672.

COVEY, H. C., & MENARD, S. (1988). Trends in elderly criminal victimization from 1973-1984. *Research on Aging, 12,* 329-341.

CROMWELL, J. B., HANNAN, M. J., LABYS, W. C., & TERRAZA, M. (1994). *Multivariate tests for time series models.* Thousand Oaks, CA: Sage.

CRONBACH, L. J., & FURBY, L. (1970). How should we measure change–Or should we? *Psychological Bulletin, 72,* 68-80.

DAVIES, R. B. (1994). From cross-sectional to longitudinal analysis. In A. Dale & R. B. Davies (Eds.), *Analyzing social and political change: A casebook of methods* (pp. 20-40). London: Sage.

DAVIES, R. B., & PICKLES, A. R. (1985). Longitudinal versus cross-sectional methods for behavioral research: A first-round knockout. *Environment and Planning A, 12,* 1315-1329.

DAVIS, J. A. (1985). *The logic of causal order.* Beverly Hills, CA: Sage.

DAVIS, J. A., & SMITH, T. W. (1992). *The NORC General Social Survey: A user's guide.* Newbury Park, CA: Sage.

DAVIS, K. (1963). The theory of change and response in modern demographic history. *Population Index, 22,* 345-366.

DEMPSTER-McCLAIN, D., & MOEN, P. (1998). Finding respondents in a follow-up study. In J. Z. Giele & G. H. Elder, Jr. (Eds.), *Methods of life course research* (pp. 128-151). Thousand Oaks, CA: Sage.

EASTERLIN, R. A. (1987). *Birth and fortune* (2nd ed.). Chicago: University of Chicago Press.

ELLIOTT, D. S., HUIZINGA, D., & AGETON, S. S. (1985). *Explaining delinquency and drug use.* Beverly Hills, CA: Sage.

ELLIOTT, D. S., HUIZINGA, D., & MENARD, S. (1989). *Multiple problem youth: Delinquency, substance use, and mental health problems.* New York: Springer-Verlag.

FEDERAL BUREAU OF INVESTIGATION. (annual). *Uniform crime reports.* Washington, DC: Government Printing Office.

FINKEL, S. E. (1995). *Causal analysis with panel data.* Thousand Oaks, CA: Sage.

FIREBAUGH, G. (1980). Cross national versus historical regression models: Conditions of equivalence in comparative analysis. *Comparative Social Research, 2,* 333-344.

86

FOWLER, F. (1998). Design and evaluation of survey questions. In L. Bickman & D. J. Rog (Eds.), *Handbook of applied social research methods* (pp. 343-374). Thousand Oaks, CA: Sage.

FREEDMAN, D., THORNTON, A., CAMBURN, D., ALWIN, D., & YOUNG-DEMARCO, L. (1988). The life history calendar: A technique for collecting retrospective data. In C. Clogg (Ed.), *Sociological methodology 1988* (pp. 37-68). Washington, DC: American Sociological Association.

FREEMAN, D. (1983). *Margaret Mead and Samoa: The making and unmaking of an anthropological myth*. Cambridge, MA: Harvard University Press.

GIELE, J. Z., & ELDER, G. H., Jr. (Eds.). (1998). *Methods of life course research: Qualitative and quantitative approaches*. Thousand Oaks, CA: Sage.

GIST, N. P., & FAVA, S. F. (1974). *Urban society* (6th ed.). New York: Crowell/Harper & Row.

GLENN, N. (1976). Cohort analysts' futile quest: Statistical attempts to separate age, period, and cohort effects. *American Sociological Review, 41,* 900-904.

GLENN, N. (1977). *Cohort analysis*. Beverly Hills, CA: Sage.

GOLD, M., & REIMER, D. J. (1975). Changing patterns of delinquent behavior among Americans 13 through 16 years old: 1967-1972. *Crime and Delinquency Literature, 2,* 483-577.

GOTTMAN, J. M. (Ed.). (1995). *The analysis of change*. Mahwah, NJ: Lawrence Erlbaum.

GRAETZ, B. (1987). Cohort changes in educational inequality. *Social Science Research, 12,* 329-344.

GRAHAM, J. W., & HOFER, S. M. (2000). Multiple imputation in multivariate research. In T. D. Little, K. U. Schnabel, & J. Baumert (Eds.), *Modeling longitudinal and multilevel data: Practical issues, applied approaches, and specific examples* (pp. 201-218). Mahwah, NJ: Lawrence Erlbaum.

GRANGER, C. W. J. (1969). Investigating causal relations by econometric models and cross-spectral methods. *Econometrica, 32,* 424-438.

GREENBERG, D. F. (1985). Age, Crime, and social explanation. *American Journal of Sociology, 91,* 1-21.

GRUSKY, D. B. (2001). *Stratification: class, race, and gender in sociological perspective* (2nd ed.). Boulder, CO: Westview.

HAMBLIN, R. L., JACOBSEN, R. B., & MILLER, J. L. L. (1973). *A mathematical theory of social change*. New York: John Wiley.

HARTFORD, R. B. (1984). The case of the elusive infant mortality rate. *Population Today, 2,* 6-7.

HAYDUK, L. A. (1987). *Structural modeling with LISREL: Essentials and advances*. Baltimore: Johns Hopkins University Press.

HEISE, D. R. (1975). *Causal analysis*. New York: John Wiley.

HENRY, B., MOFFITT, T. E., CASPI, A., LANGLEY, J., & SILVA, P. A. (1994). On the "remembrance of things past": A longitudinal evaluation of the retrospective method. *Psychological Assessment, 2,* 92-101.

HEYNS, B. (1978). *Summer learning and the effects of schooling*. New York: Academic Press.

HILL, M. S. (1992). *The Panel Study of Income Dynamics: A user's guide*. Newbury Park, CA: Sage.

HOBCRAFT, J., MENKEN, J., & PRESTON, S. (1982). Age, period, and cohort effects in demography: A review. *Population Index, 42,* 4-43.

HOGAN, H., & ROBINSON, G. (2000). *What the Census Bureau's coverage evaluation programs tell us about the differential undercount*. Washington, DC: U.S. Department of Commerce, Bureau of the Census.

HOSMER, D. W., Jr., & LEMESHOW, S. (1999). *Applied survival analysis: Regression modeling of time to event data*. New York: John Wiley.

HOUT, M. (1983). *Mobility tables*. Beverly Hills, CA: Sage.

HOUT, M., MANZA, J., & BROOKS, C. (1999). Classes, unions, and the realignment of U.S. presidential voting, 1952-1992. In G. Evans (Ed.), *The end of class politics: Class voting in comparative perspective* (pp. 83-95). Oxford, UK: Oxford University Press.

HUCKFELDT, R. R., KOHFELD, C. W., & LIKENS, T. W. (1982). *Dynamic modeling: An introduction*. Beverly Hills, CA: Sage.

HUIZINGA, D. H., MENARD, S., & ELLIOTT, D. S. (1989). Delinquency and drug use: Temporal and developmental patterns. *Justice Quarterly, 2,* 419-455.

INGLEHART, R. (1997). *Modernization and postmodernization: Cultural, economic, and political change in 43 societies*. Princeton, NJ: Princeton University Press.

JENKINS, G. M., & WATTS, D. G. (1968). *Spectral analysis and its applications*. San Francisco: Holden-Day.

JOHNSTON, L. D., BACHMAN, J. G., & O'MALLEY, P. M. (annual). *Monitoring the future: Questionnaire responses from the nation's high school seniors*. Ann Arbor, MI: Institute for Social Research.

JÖRESKOG, K. G., & SÖRBOM, D. (1989). *LISREL 2: A guide to the program and applications* (2nd ed.). Chicago: SPSS.

KALTON, G., KASPRZYK, D., & McMILLEN, D. B. (1989). Nonsampling errors in panel surveys. In D. G. Kasprzyk, G. Duncan, G. Kalton, & M. P. Singh (Eds.), *Panel surveys* (pp. 249-270). New York: John Wiley.

KANDEL, D. B. (1975). Stages of adolescent involvement in drug use. *Science, 192,* 912-914.

KANDEL, D. B., & FAUST, R. (1975). Sequence and states in patterns of adolescent drug use. *Archives of General Psychiatry, 32,* 923-932.

KANDEL, D. B., & LOGAN, J. A. (1984). Patterns of drug use from adolescence to young adulthood: I. Periods of risk for initiation, continued use, and discontinuation. *American Journal of Public Health, 72,* 660-666.

KAPLAN, D. (2000). *Structural equation modeling: Foundations and extensions*. Thousand Oaks, CA: Sage.

KELLING, G. L., PATE, T., DIECKMAN, D. E., & BROWN, C. E. (1974). *The Kansas City Preventative Patrol Experiment: A summary report*. Washington, DC: Police Foundation.

KERLINGER, F. N. (1986). *Foundations of behavioral research* (3rd ed.). New York: Holt, Rinehart & Winston.

KESSLER, R. C., & GREENBERG, D. F. (1981). *Linear panel analysis: Models of quantitative change*. New York: John Wiley.

KIM, K. H., & ROUSH, F. W. (1980). *Mathematics for social scientists*. New York: Elsevier.

KNOKE, D., & HOUT, M. (1976). Reply to Glenn. *American Sociological Review, 41,* 905-908.

KRAEMER, H. C., & THIEMANN, S. (1987). *How many subjects? Statistical power analysis in research*. Newbury Park, CA: Sage.

LAGRANGE, R. L., & WHITE, H. R. (1985). Age differences in delinquency: A test of a theory. *Criminology, 22,* 19-45.

LANGEHEINE, R., & VAN DE POL, F. (1994). Discrete-time mixed Markov latent class models. In A. Dale & R. B. Davies (Eds.), *Analyzing social and political change: A casebook of methods* (pp. 170-197). London: Sage.

LEHNEN, R. G., & SKOGAN, W. G. (Eds.). (1981). *The National Crime Survey: Working papers: Vol. I. Current and historical perspectives*. Washington, DC: U.S. Department of Justice.

LEPKOWSKI, J. M. (1989). Treatment of wave nonresponse in panel surveys. In D. G. Kasprzyk, G. Duncan, G. Kalton, & M. P. Singh (Eds.), *Panel surveys* (pp. 348-374). New York: John Wiley.

LEWIS, O. (1951). *Life in a Mexican village: Tepoztlan restudied*. Urbana: University of Illinois Press.

88

LIKER, J. K., AUGUSTYNIAK, S., & DUNCAN, G. J. (1985). Panel data and models of change: A comparison of first difference and conventional two-wave models. *Social Science Research, 12,* 80-101.

LITTLE, R. J. A., & SU, H. (1989). Item nonresponse in panel surveys. In D. Kasprzyk, G. J. Duncan, G. Kalton, & M. P. Singh (Eds.), *Panel surveys* (pp. 400-425). New York: John Wiley.

LITTLE, T. D., SCHNABEL, K. U., & BAUMERT, J. (Eds.). (2000). *Modeling longitudinal and multilevel data: Practical issues, applied approaches, and specific examples.* Mahwah, NJ: Lawrence Erlbaum.

LLOYD, L., ARMOUR, P. K., & SMITH, R. J. (1987). Suicide in Texas: A cohort analysis of trends in suicide rates, 1945-1980. *Suicide and Life-Threatening Behavior, 12,* 205-217.

MAHAJAN, V., & PETERSON, R. A. (1985). *Models for innovation diffusion.* Beverly Hills, CA: Sage.

MARKUS, G. B. (1979). *Analyzing panel data.* Beverly Hills, CA: Sage.

MARSDEN, P. V. (Ed.). (1991). *Sociological methodology 1991.* Washington, DC: American Sociological Association.

MARTIN, E. (1983). Surveys as social indicators: Problems in monitoring trends. In P. H. Rossi, J. D. Wright, & A. B. Anderson (Eds.), *Handbook of survey research* (pp. 677-743). Orlando, FL: Academic Press.

MASON, K. O., MASON, W. M., WINSBOROUGH, H. H., & POOLE, W. K. (1973). Some methodological issues in cohort analysis of archival data. *American Sociological Review, 32,* 242-258.

MASON, W. M., MASON, K. O., & WINSBOROUGH, H. H. (1976). Reply to Glenn. *American Sociological Review, 41,* 904-905.

MAULDIN, W. P., & BERELSON, B. (1978). Conditions of fertility decline in developing countries: 1965-1975. *Studies in Family Planning, 2,* 89-145.

McARDLE, J. J., & BELL, R. Q. (2000). An introduction to latent growth curve models for developmental data analysis. In T. D. Little, K. U. Schnabel, & J. Baumert (Eds.), *Modeling longitudinal and multilevel data* (pp. 69-107). Mahwah, NJ: Lawrence Erlbaum.

McCORD, J. (1983). A longitudinal study of aggression and antisocial behavior. In K. T. Van Dusen & S. A. Mednick (Eds.), *Prospective studies of crime and delinquency* (pp. 269-275). Boston: Kluwer-Nijhoff.

McGINNIS, R. (1968). A stochastic theory of social mobility. *American Sociological Review, 23,* 712-722.

McKEOWN, T. (1976). *The modern rise of population.* London: Edward Arnold.

McKEOWN, T., & RECORD, R. (1962). Reasons for the decline of mortality in England and Wales during the 19th century. *Population Studies, 12,* 94-122.

McKIM, V. R., & TURNER, S. P. (Eds.). (1997). Causality in crisis? Statistical methods and the search for causal knowledge in the social sciences. Notre Dame, IN: Notre Dame University Press.

McNEILL, W. H. (1976). *Plagues and peoples.* New York: Anchor/Doubleday.

MEAD, M. (1928). *Coming of age in Western Samoa: A psychological study of primitive youth for western civilization.* New York: William Morrow.

MENARD, S. (1983, April). *Reliability issues in international comparisons of inequality of income.* Paper presented at the annual meeting of the Western Social Science Association, San Diego, CA.

MENARD, S. (1986). A research note on international comparisons of inequality of income. *Social Forces, 2,* 778-793.

MENARD, S. (1987a). Fertility, development, and family planning, 1970-1982: An analysis of cases weighted by population. *Studies in Comparative International Development, 22,* 103-127.

MENARD, S. (1987b). Short term trends in crime and delinquency: A comparison of UCR, NCS, and self-report data. *Justice Quarterly, 2,* 455-474.

MENARD, S., & ELLIOTT, D. S. (1990a). Longitudinal and cross-sectional data collection and analysis in the study of crime and delinquency. *Justice Quarterly, 2,* 11-55.

MENARD, S., & ELLIOTT, D. S. (1990b). Self-reported offending, maturational reform, and the Easterlin hypothesis. *Journal of Quantitative Criminology, 2,* 237-267.

MENARD, S., & ELLIOTT, D. S. (1994). Delinquent bonding, moral beliefs, and illegal behavior: A three-wave panel model. *Justice Quarterly, 11,* 173-188.

MENARD, S., ELLIOTT, D. S., & HUIZINGA, D. (1989). *The dynamics of deviant behavior: A national survey progress report* (National Youth Survey Report No. 49). Boulder, CO: Institute of Behavioral Science.

MENARD, S., & HUIZINGA, D. (1989). Age, period, and cohort size effects on self-reported alcohol, marijuana, and polydrug use: Results from the National Youth Survey. *Social Science Research, 12,* 174-194.

MENARD, S., & MIHALIC, S. (2001). The tripartite conceptual framework in adolescence and adulthood: Evidence from a national sample. *Journal of Drug Issues, 31,* 905-938.

MENSCH, B. S., & KANDEL, D. B. (1988). Underreporting of substance use in a national longitudinal youth cohort: Individual and interviewer effects. *Public Opinion Quarterly, 52,* 100-124.

MURRAY, G. F., & ERICKSON, P. G. (1987). Cross-sectional versus longitudinal research: An empirical comparison of projected and subsequent criminality. *Social Science Research, 12,* 107-118.

NAGEL, E. (1961). *The structure of science.* New York: Harcourt, Brace, & World.

NAMBOODIRI, K., & SUCHINDRAN, C. M. (1987). *Life table techniques and their applications.* Orlando, FL: Academic Press.

NEWCOMB, M. D., & BENTLER, P. M. (1988). *Consequences of adolescent drug use: Impact on the lives of young adults.* Newbury Park, CA: Sage.

NOTESTEIN, F. W. (1945). Population: The long view. In T. W. Schultz (Ed.), *Food for the world* (pp. 26-57). Chicago: University of Chicago Press.

OSTROM, C. W., Jr. (1990). *Time series analysis: Regression techniques.* Newbury Park, CA: Sage.

PALMORE, E. (1978). When can age, period, and cohort be separated? *Social Forces, 52,* 282-295.

PATTERSON, G. R. (1995). Orderly change in a stable world: The antisocial trait as a chimera. In J. M. Gottman (Ed.), *The analysis of change* (pp. 83-101). Mahwah, NJ: Lawrence Erlbaum.

PAYNE, C., PAYNE, J., & HEATH, A. (1994). Modelling trends in multi-way tables. In A. Dale & R. B. Davies (Eds.), *Analyzing social and political change: A casebook of methods* (pp. 43-74). London: Sage.

PEARL, J. (2000). *Causality: Models, reasoning, and inference.* Cambridge, UK: Cambridge University Press.

PETERS, H. E. (1988). Retrospective versus panel data in analyzing lifecycle events. *Journal of Human Resources, 22,* 488-573.

PIAGET, J. (1948). *The moral judgment of the child.* New York: Free Press.

PIAGET, J. (1951). *The child's conception of the world.* New York: Humanities Press.

PIAGET, J. (1952). *The origins of intelligence in children.* New York: International University Press.

PLATT, J. R. (1964). Strong inference. *Science, 142,* 347-353.

PLEWIS, I. (1985). *Analyzing change: Measurement and explanation using longitudinal data.* Chichester, UK: Wiley.

POPULATION REFERENCE BUREAU. (1989). Speaking graphically: When did you say you were born, Miss? *Population Today, 2,* 2.

PRESIDENT'S COMMISSION ON LAW ENFORCEMENT AND THE ADMINISTRATION OF JUSTICE. (1967). *The challenge of crime in a free society.* Washington, DC: Government Printing Office.

RAUDENBUSH, S. W. (1995). Hierarchical linear models to study the effects of social context on development. In J. M. Gottman (Ed.), *The analysis of change* (pp. 165-201). Mahwah, NJ: Lawrence Erlbaum.

RAUDENBUSH, S. W. (2001). Toward a coherent framework for comparing trajectories of individual change. In L. M. Collins & A. G. Sayer (Eds.), *New methods for the analysis of change* (pp. 35-64). Washington, DC: American Psychological Association.

RAUDENBUSH, S. W., & BRYK, A. S. (2002). *Hierarchical linear models: Applications and data analysis methods* (2nd ed.). Thousand Oaks, CA: Sage.

RAUDENBUSH, S., BRYK, A., CHEONG, Y. F., & CONGDON, R. (2000). *HLM 2: Hierarchical linear and nonlinear modeling.* Chicago: Scientific Software International.

REDFIELD, R. (1930). *Tepoztlan: A Mexican village.* Chicago: University of Chicago Press.

RENNISON, C. M. (2000). *Criminal victimization 1992: Changes 1998-99 with trends 1993-99.* Washington, DC: U.S. Department of Justice.

RICHARDSON, L. F. (1960). *Arms and insecurity.* Pittsburgh: Boxwood Press.

ROBEY, B. (1989). Two hundred years and counting: The 1990 census. *Population Bulletin, 4*(1), 1-43.

RODGERS, W. L. (1982a). Estimable functions of age, period, and cohort effects. *American Sociological Review, 42,* 774-787.

RODGERS, W. L. (1982b). Reply to comment by Smith, Mason, and Fienberg. *American Sociological Review, 42,* 793-796.

ROGOSA, D. (1995). Myths and methods: "Myths about longitudinal research" plus supplemental questions. In J. M. Gottman (Ed.), *The analysis of change* (pp. 3-66). Mahwah, NJ: Lawrence Erlbaum.

ROITBERG, T., & MENARD, S. (1995). Adolescent violence: A test of integrated theory. *Studies on Crime and Crime Prevention, 2,* 177-196.

ROSSI, P. H., FREEMAN, H. E., & LIPSEY, M. W. (1999). *Evaluation: A systematic approach* (6th ed.). Newbury Park, CA: Sage.

ROSTOW, W. W. (1960). *The stages of economic growth: A non-communist manifesto.* Cambridge, UK: Cambridge University Press.

ROVINE, M. J., & DELANEY, M. (1990). Missing data estimation in developmental research. In A. von Eye (Ed.), *Statistical methods in longitudinal research: Vol. I. Principles and structuring change* (pp. 35-79). Boston: Academic Press.

RUBIN, Z., & MITCHELL, C. (1978). Couples research as couples counseling: Some unintended effects of studying close relationships. *American Psychologist, 31,* 17-25.

RUTTER, M., MAUGHAN, B., PICKLES, A., & SIMONOFF, E. (1998). Retrospective recall recalled. In R. B. Cairns, L. R. Bergman, & J. Kagan (Eds.), *Methods and models for studying the individual* (pp. 219-242). Thousand Oaks, CA: Sage.

RYDER, N. B. (1965). The cohort as a concept in the study of social change. *American Sociological Review, 32,* 843-861.

SANDERS, D., & WARD, H. (1994). Time-series techniques for repeated cross-section data. In A. Dale & R. B. Davies (Eds.), *Analyzing social and political change* (pp. 201-223). London: Sage.

SAYRS, L. W. (1989). *Pooled time series analysis.* Newbury Park, CA: Sage.

SCHMIDT, P., & WITTE, A. D. (1988). *Predicting recidivism using survival models.* New York: Springer-Verlag.

SCHOENBERG, R. (1977). Dynamic models and cross-sectional data: The consequences of dynamic misspecification. *Social Science Research, 2,* 133-144.

SCHWEINHART, L. J., & WEIKART, D. P. (1980). *Young children grow up: The effects of the Perry Preschool Program on youths through age 15*. Ypsilanti, MI: High/Scope Educational Research Foundation.

SHAFFER, J. P. (Ed.). (1992). *The role of models in nonexperimental social science: Two debates*. Washington, DC: American Educational Research Association and American Statistical Association.

SHELDON, E. B., & MOORE, W. E. (Eds.). (1968). *Indicators of social change: Concepts and measurements*. New York: Russell Sage.

SHRYOCK, H. S., SIEGEL, J., & Associates. (1976). *The methods and materials of demography* (Condensed ed. by E. G. Stockwell). New York: Academic Press.

SIMON, H. J. (1954). Spurious correlation: A causal interpretation. *Journal of the American Statistical Association, 42*, 467-479.

SIMS, C. A. (1972). Money, income, and causality. *American Economic Review, 62*, 540-552.

SKOGAN, W. G. (1976). The victims of crime: Some national survey findings. In A. L. Guenther (Ed.), *Criminal behavior and social systems* (2nd ed., pp. 131-148). Chicago: Rand McNally.

SMITH, H. L., MASON, W. M., & FIENBERG, S. E. (1982). More chimeras of the age-period-cohort accounting framework: Comment on Rodgers. *American Sociological Review, 42*, 787-793.

SNIJDERS, T., & BOSKER, R. (1999). *Multilevel analysis: An introduction to basic and advanced multilevel modeling*. London: Sage.

SORENSON, A. M., BROWNFIELD, D., & CARLSON, V. (1989). Adult reports of juvenile delinquency: A research note on the reliability of a retrospective design. *Sociological Spectrum, 2*, 227-237.

STOOLMILLER, M. (1995). Using latent growth curve models to study developmental processes. In J. M. Gottman (Ed.), *The analysis of change* (pp. 103-138). Mahwah, NJ: Lawrence Erlbaum.

STOOLMILLER, M., & BANK, L. (1995). Autoregressive effects in structural equation models: We see some problems. In J. M. Gottman (Ed.), *The analysis of change* (pp. 261-276). Mahwah, NJ: Lawrence Erlbaum.

TARIS, T. W. (2000). *A primer in longitudinal data analysis*. London: Sage.

THOMLINSON, R. (1976). *Population dynamics: Causes and consequences of world population change* (2nd ed.). New York: Random House.

THOMPSON, W. S. (1929). Population. *American Journal of Sociology, 32*, 959-975.

THOMSEN, D. E. (1987). In the beginning was quantum mechanics: Cosmologists take a chance on a quantum universe. *Science News, 131*, 346-347.

THORNBERRY, T. P., BJERREGAARD, B., & MILES, W. (1993). The consequences of respondent attrition in panel studies: A simulation based on the Rochester Youth Development Study. *Journal of Quantitative Criminology, 2*, 127-158.

TOLNAY, S. E., & CHRISTENSON, R. L. (1984). The effects of social setting and family planning programs on recent fertility declines in developing countries: A reassessment. *Sociology and Social Research, 62*, 72-89.

TSUI, A. O., & BOGUE, D. J. (1978). Declining world fertility: Trends, causes, implications. *Population Bulletin, 33*(4), 2-55.

U.S. BUREAU OF THE CENSUS. (1975). *Historical statistics of the United States: Colonial times to 1970* (Bicentennial ed.). Washington, DC: Government Printing Office.

VAN DE WALLE, E., & KNODEL, J. (1980). Europe's fertility transition: New evidence and lessons for today's developing world. *Population Bulletin, 34*(6), 2-40.

VIGDERHOUS, G. (1977). Forecasting sociological phenomena: Application of Box-Jenkins methodology to suicide rates. In K. F. Schuessler (Ed.), *Sociological methodology 1978* (pp. 20-51). San Francisco: Jossey-Bass.

92

WALL, W. D., & WILLIAMS, H. L. (1970). *Longitudinal studies and the social sciences.* London: Heinemann.

WALTON, M. A., RAMANATHAN, C. S., & REISCHL, T. M. (1998). Tracking substance abusers in longitudinal research: Understanding follow-up contact difficulty. *American Journal of Community Psychology, 22,* 233-253.

WEI, W. W. S. (1990). *Time series analysis: Univariate and multivariate methods.* Redwood City, CA: Addison-Wesley.

WEIKART, D. P., BOND, J. T., & McNEIL, J. T. (1978). *The Ypsilanti Perry Preschool Project: Preschool years and longitudinal results through fourth grade.* Ypsilanti, MI: High/Scope Educational Research Foundation.

WEIS, J. G. (1986). Issues in the measurement of criminal careers. In A. Blumstein, J. Cohen, J. A. Roth, & C. A. Visher (Eds.), *Criminal careers and "career criminals"* (Vol. II, pp. 1-51). Washington, DC: National Academy Press.

WETZEL, R. D., REICH, T., MURPHY, G. E., PROVINCE, M., & MILLER, J. P. (1987). The changing relationship between age and suicide rates: Cohort effect, period effect, or both? *Psychiatric Developments, 2,* 174-218.

WILLIAMS, J., & GOLD, M. (1972). From delinquent behavior to official delinquency. *Social Problems, 22,* 209-229.

WOFFORD, S. (1989). *A preliminary analysis of the relationship between employment and delinquency/crime for adolescents and young adults* (National Youth Survey Report No. 50). Boulder, CO: Institute of Behavioral Science.

WRIGHT, R. E. (1989). The Easterlin hypothesis and European fertility rates. *Population and Development Review, 12,* 107-122.

WRIGHT, R. E., & MAXIM, P. S. (1987). Canadian fertility trends: A further test of the Easterlin hypothesis. *Canadian Review of Sociology and Anthropology, 22,* 339-357.

YAFFEE, R. (with McGEE, M.). (2000). *An introduction to time series analysis and forecasting with applications of SAS and SPSS.* San Diego: Academic Press.

YAMAGUCHI, K. (1991). *Event history analysis.* Newbury Park, CA: Sage.

YAMAGUCHI, K., & KANDEL, D. B. (1984a). Patterns of drug use from adolescence to young adulthood: II. Sequences of progression. *American Journal of Public Health, 72,* 668-672.

YAMAGUCHI, K., & KANDEL, D. B. (1984b). Patterns of drug use from adolescence to young adulthood: III. Predictors of progression. *American Journal of Public Health, 72,* 673-681.

ZELLER, R. A., & CARMINES, E. G. (1980). *Measurement in the social sciences: The link between theory and data.* Cambridge, UK: Cambridge University Press.

ABOUT THE AUTHOR

Scott Menard is a Research Associate in the Institute of Behavioral Science at the University of Colorado, Boulder. He received his Ph.D. from the University of Colorado in 1981. His publications include *Perspectives on Population* (with Elizabeth W. Moen), *Multiple Problem Youth* (with Delbert S. Elliott and David Huizinga), *Juvenile Gangs* (with Herbert C. Covey and Robert J. Franzese), and *Applied Logistic Regression Analysis* (Sage Publications, 2002), as well as papers on demography and development, crime and delinquency, and statistics. His present research interests focus on the analysis of the transition from adolescence to adulthood, including the impact of adolescent experiences and behaviors on adult outcomes.